# HOW TO ADOPT A CHILD FROM ANOTHER COUNTRY

# HOW TO ADOPT A CHILD FROM ANOTHER COUNTRY

Eileen M. Wirth &
Joan Worden

ABINGDON PRESS
Nashville

HOW TO ADOPT A CHILD FROM ANOTHER COUNTRY

Copyright © 1993 by Abingdon Press

This book is printed on recycled, acid-free paper.

**Library of Congress Cataloging-in-Publication Data**

WIRTH, EILEEN, 1947-
 How to adopt a child from another country  /  Eileen Wirth, Joan Worden.
  p.    cm.
 Includes bibliographical references.
 ISBN 0-687-00772-0 (alk. paper)
  1. Intercountry adoption—United States.    I. Worden, Joan, 1937-
II. Title.
HV875.5.W57     1993
362.7'34—dc20
                                                          92-13018
                                                              CIP

Scripture quotations are from the New Revised Standard Version of the Bible, copyright 1989 by the Division of Christian Education of the National Council of the Churches of Christ in the USA. Used by permission.

MANUFACTURED IN THE UNITED STATES OF AMERICA

To our wonderful families—
*Ron, Raj,* and *Shanti Psota;*
*Ray,*
*Randy,*
*Bob,*
*Raelynn,*
*Mindy,*
and
*Jodi Worden*

# CONTENTS

# CHAPTER 1

# An Introduction to Foreign Adoption

This is a book of hope for people who wonder if the child they long for can ever be theirs. It is written in love by two people who have traveled that long and painful road to a successful conclusion—and have stayed around to help others embark on the journey.

It is also written to the relatives and friends of those who must travel this road. We know that you also suffer. Your love, encouragement, and care are needed.

Finally, it is written to children who were born elsewhere and adopted by Americans, especially to our own children. Sometimes it is difficult to be an adopted child. We hope that this book helps you understand how you became part of our lives and what your adoptive parents experienced before you did.

Only someone who has ever wanted a child and been unable to have one can quite understand the special pain involved. Today many of these people are successful two-income couples or successful single people leading seemingly perfect lives. Few would guess the core of emptiness they face.

We've known some couples who spent a small fortune on medical treatments that virtually took over their lives. We've known others who settled into a sort of quiet despair because they had heard how difficult it is to adopt or had been told by several agencies that they were too old, of different religions, divorced, or simply not top-of-the-list prospects.

To such people we say: don't give up. Take another look at the process of foreign adoption. You may find the child of your life just waiting in Asia, Eastern Europe, or Latin America.

This book is both a guide in how to succeed in foreign adoption and the personal story of our adoptions along with those of several other people. It includes never-before-published material on how Korean adoptees can reunite with their birth families, and it looks at current issues in adoption, such as adoptions from Eastern Europe and single-parent adoptions. It includes a list of agencies in each state to contact about foreign adoption.

You need such information, but you also need to know that foreign adoption works. That's why we will tell you our own stories and those of other people. We'll guide you down the paths we've helped many others follow.

We know there are people all over the country who need this information because both of us have received many unlikely calls from people we've never met or heard of, asking what they can do to adopt.

As a starter, forget much of what you've read or heard about adoption. There are many myths. We want to help you understand what happens before, during, and after a foreign adoption. We'll try to anticipate your questions:

- Do I want to adopt?
- Is foreign adoption for us (or me, if you're single)?
- How do I get started?
- How do I decide which country to apply for?
- How do I find an agency?
- Do we qualify?
- Can we afford to do this?
- What happens when my child arrives?
- How will people react?
- How do I raise a foreign-born child?

Many Americans tend to view adoption as a "second best" form of parenthood. Nothing could be further from the truth. An adoptive child is your "real child" as surely as love and concern are "real." You will be that child's "real" parent as surely as your relatives and friends are parents of their birth children.

You'll be just as proud when your child stars in the school play or scores a goal in soccer. You'll be just as irritated when your child has to be reminded for the nineteenth time to clean her room or do her homework. You'll be just as worried when your son is late getting home and just as touched when a small hand reaches for yours and a little voice says, "You're the best mommy in the whole world."

Adoption is simply another way of building a family—a very happy, beautiful, natural way. You may be amazed at how much your adoptive children come to resemble you and your relatives. Never mind that their skins may be darker or their eyes a different shape. You'll see traces of Uncle Mark just as you would in a birth child.

The road to adoption can be long and difficult. You must expect obstacles. But at the end, the reward is beyond measure for those who take the risk to hope and love. We invite you to explore that journey.

Before we begin, two notes are in order: (1) Although adoption workers can be either male or female, we use female pronouns because the vast majority are women; (2) Our stories are in chapters 16 and 17. However, to introduce ourselves, we are:

- *Joan Worden,* who with her husband, Ray, adopted Korean daughters Mindy and Jodi, and then became a social worker specializing in foreign adoption. Her family also includes three biological children—Randy, Bob, and Raelynn.

- *Eileen Wirth,* mother of son Raj from India and daughter Shanti from Thailand. A journalist by trade, she and her husband Ron Psota, a former Peace Corps volunteer in India, became foreign-adoption volunteers after adopting the children.

We're fairly ordinary people who started our journeys to adoption about where you probably are now. We learned a lot through trial and error. We worried that we wouldn't meet agency standards or that something terrible would happen. To this day we aren't perfect mothers or perfect anything. But we and our families came through the adoption process stronger, wiser, and much happier. We're betting that many of you will too.

CHAPTER 2

# An Adoption Quiz

Could I really hope to adopt?

If you've been secretly asking yourself this question, chances are excellent that you've already made a subconscious decision to do so. Your heart knows you want to, but your head hasn't quite caught up with it. And the part of you that desperately wants to adopt is too afraid even to hope because you've heard repeatedly how difficult it is, how long the waits are, and how few children there are.

Be of good cheer. This is an excellent way to start the adoptive process. You're right where thousands of families with happy stories were just a few short years ago.

As a start on our Road to Adoption, we suggest that you take the following quiz—then see how you compare with parents who are likely to end up adopting children. A word to the wise: the "correct" answers may not be the ones you think you are supposed to pick. Be honest with yourself.

## ADOPTION QUIZ

1. I really love being around children.

   True_____

   False_____

2. My husband and I are in total agreement about adopting.

   True_____

   False_____

3. I want to adopt because there are so many children in the world who need to be rescued from terrible conditions.

   True_____

   False_____

4. I'm absolutely sure I'd be a great parent.

   True_____

   False_____

5. I have no concerns about what other people might think when they see me with a child whose looks differ from mine.

   True_____

   False_____

6. I'm scared to death of this thing, but I know I have to do it.

   True_____

   False_____

7. I just know that somewhere in this world there's a child for me, and I have to find him or her.

   True_____

   False_____

8. I know this won't be easy, but if other people can adopt, then so can I.

   True_____

   False_____

9. I want this so badly, but I'm terrified of the process. What if we are rejected and I have to give up my dream?

   True_____

   False_____

10. I'm scared that the adoption worker will find out something terrible about me that I don't even know myself.

   True_____

   False_____

## ANSWERS

Nearly everyone starts an adoption with some ambivalence. If your answers to most questions reflect that state of mind, you're perfectly normal. While there are no right or wrong answers to these questions, here are our comments on each.

### 1. I REALLY LOVE BEING AROUND CHILDREN.

Either true or false is an acceptable answer to this question. Some people are born with a gift for children, especially small children. Kindergarten teachers are surely one of God's gifts to the world. If you are one of the fortunate souls who can answer a wholehearted "true" to this question because you have experience with children and honestly enjoy them, your road to adoption may be easier than that of many people who haven't spent time with children.

Eileen, for example, used to secretly wonder how parents endured their children. She was basically uneasy around children. They were messy, got tired and cranky, fought with each other, and took over perfectly satisfactory grown-up lives. They were always interrupting the most interesting adult conversations. Her experience in leading a 4-H group was just short of disastrous. She had bombed as a tutor to a slow-learning boy. She had rarely baby-sat except for her brothers, and all she could recall was that they wouldn't obey her.

Yet the time came when she knew beyond all knowing that she had to have children. It might be torture and she might hate every minute of it, but the awful feeling that she *had* to do this was torture too. A week before her son, Raj, arrived from India, she was terrified that she wouldn't like him and he would not like her.

Eileen was shocked by her reaction to motherhood. *She loved it.* She adored Raj on sight. He instantly became the joy of her life. She realized now why her heart had insisted she do this. The terrible, tormenting emptiness vanished.

She also discovered that living with a child full-time is much easier than occasionally visiting one. She never minded the work, the sudden loss of freedom, or the exhaustion of taking care of a baby. This was the most wonderful thing that had ever happened to her, and up to the day Raj came, she had been afraid she might not be a very good mother.

In short, if your heart is telling you loudly that you're missing something by not having a child in your life, listen to it. *Listen to it. Listen to it.*

## 2. MY HUSBAND AND I ARE IN TOTAL AGREEMENT ABOUT ADOPTING.

Either true or false is an acceptable answer to this question. It is very common for one partner, usually the wife, to be much more determined to adopt than the other. Agencies see this all the time. Ideally, the reluctant partner is merely reluctant, not openly opposed to adoption.

Adoption is the most important decision that most couples will ever make. They both must be able to live with it, but both don't have to be initially enthusiastic. If one of you is uncertain, it may help to know that the arrival of a child usually changes this uncertainty (which may be a mask for fear) into delight, even adoration.

Couples expecting a biological child also often feel a combination of joy, hope, fear, and dread. They, like prospective adoptive parents, know that a child means added responsibility and expense. They know they will lose much of their freedom. It would be surprising if the additional difficulties and uncertainties connected with adoption did not magnify these normal fears and concerns. Open communication between husband and wife concerning reasons for the uncertainty can help resolve difficulties.

## 3. I WANT TO ADOPT BECAUSE THERE ARE SO MANY CHILDREN IN THE WORLD WHO NEED TO BE RESCUED FROM TERRIBLE CONDITIONS.

If you answered "true," we suggest you look long and hard at your motives. We can't stress too strongly that you should never adopt any child to rescue him or her. Strange as it may sound, you should adopt a child for selfish reasons:

- You feel you are missing something important in life by not having children.
- You think a child will make your life happier.
- You think you will enjoy being a parent.
- You enjoy being a parent, but don't believe you should have any more biological children.

If you adopt a child to rescue him or her, you'll wear your son or daughter like a martyr's crown. No child should ever have to bear that burden. You wouldn't like it and neither will any child.

When Eileen and her husband, Ron, adopted Raj they found out that only one question on the lengthy questionnaire they filled out for Mother Teresa had counted: Why did they want to adopt from India? Eileen's response stressing Ron's Peace Corps service in India and their cultural ties with India was acceptable. A response indicating a desire to "save suffering humanity" might have eliminated them.

Since you might have thought you were *supposed* to answer "true," don't count yourself out if you did. But think twice. The only reason to adopt is that you want to become a parent.

Incidentally, one of the fastest ways to turn off people who have already adopted foreign-born children is to praise them for their nobility. They didn't adopt to be noble—or they shouldn't have. The vast majority feel lucky to have their children. They're likely to almost assault you with photos of their children long after most parents have stopped carrying snapshots.

16

## 4. I'M ABSOLUTELY SURE I'D BE A GREAT PARENT.

Either "true" or "false" may be correct answers depending on how much experience you've had with children. When Joan adopted Mindy she already had three biological children. She knew she was a good mother. She knew she could handle children. If you already have biological children or other experience in working with children, you may feel like Joan—and you're lucky.

Many people who have never had children, however, are uncertain about their ability to handle the responsibility, especially if both work full-time. They don't know if they will be good parents. They may even imagine that raising children is almost a superhuman task.

Relax. Unless there is something that would be likely to make you a poor parent, chances are you'll manage about as well as most people. If you talk to friends who are having biological children, you'll probably find that most of them have similar concerns. Like them, you will have to reorder your priorities and arrange for child care if you continue working outside the home. This is what the great bulk of American families having or adopting children do. Many new parents discover, somewhat to their surprise, that reordering priorities is not painful. Their interests change radically and spending time with their child is what they most want to do.

The best clue about your likely ability to parent is how well or poorly your parents handled your upbringing. Consciously or unconsciously, you'll probably find yourself imitating them.

## 5. I HAVE NO CONCERNS ABOUT WHAT OTHER PEOPLE MIGHT THINK WHEN THEY SEE ME WITH A CHILD WHOSE LOOKS DIFFER FROM MINE.

You probably think you should answer "true" to this question, but that would be honest only in a few cases. Eileen and Ron had spent years socializing with refugees and foreign students. They were used to being the only white Americans in crowds of foreigners. This is unusual.

Most middle-class white Americans associate primarily with other middle-class whites and don't know how they would react to this situation. It is natural to have concerns about how others might react to you and your child. Don't let these concerns deter you. There are ways to prepare yourself, which we will discuss in chapter 4.

### 6. I'M SCARED TO DEATH OF THIS THING, BUT I KNOW I HAVE TO DO IT.

If you answered "true," you'll probably end up adopting. Most successful adoptive parents *are* scared but refuse to let their fears interfere with the task to be accomplished. With foreign adoptions, there is no substitute for determination.

Both of us experienced this sentiment very strongly as did the other adoptive parents you will meet in this book. It carried all of us through many trials, setbacks, and traumas. No matter what happened, we knew we were going to win.

If you have a strong sense that a decision has been made, almost beyond or against your will, take action as soon as you finish this book. We can almost guarantee that you'll succeed in adopting.

### 7. I JUST KNOW THAT SOMEWHERE IN THIS WORLD THERE'S A CHILD FOR ME, AND I HAVE TO FIND HIM OR HER.

This statement is almost a corollary to Question 6. If you answered "true" to both, your chances of succeeding are very high. Joan can tell almost immediately which applicants have this overriding sense that they *need* to adopt because there's a special child waiting for them somewhere.

Illogical as it may seem, if you feel this way, chances are it's true. Many aspects of adoption defy conventional logic as you will see in every adoption story in this book. This is one of them.

### 8. I KNOW THIS WON'T BE EASY, BUT IF OTHER PEOPLE CAN ADOPT, THEN SO CAN I.

Again, a "true" answer indicates a likelihood you will succeed because you won't accept failure. Success in foreign adoption isn't like winning the lottery. Victory goes to those who won't give up.

### 9. I WANT THIS SO BADLY, BUT I'M TERRIFIED OF THE PROCESS. WHAT IF WE ARE REJECTED AND I HAVE TO GIVE UP MY DREAM?

Adoption is a scary prospect and a scary process. One of the hardest phone calls any adoptive parent ever makes is to a friend who has adopted or to an adoption agency. If you answered "true" you're in good company. We hope this book takes some of the terror out of that first call by telling you how to make it and what to expect as you go through the process (see chapters 3 and 6 especially).

We suggest that you set deadlines for making those calls. You'll feel better, and it is the only way to get started. There are many potential avenues to adoption. If the first few don't work, don't give up your dream—just keep trying.

It is no reflection on you if an adoption contact turns you down. Agencies serve targeted populations. Keep looking for an agency.

**10. I'M SCARED THAT THE ADOPTION WORKER WILL FIND OUT SOMETHING TERRIBLE ABOUT ME THAT I DON'T EVEN KNOW MYSELF.**

Fear is a normal part of the adoption process. A "true" answer probably means you're being honest. Most people who have adopted find the scrutiny of the home study unpleasant and invasive. If you talk to half a dozen people who have adopted, you'll probably hear half a dozen stories about how they tried to hide what they thought a social worker might see as weaknesses or defects. Joan tries to put people at ease during home studies because she knows how they feel. Not all social workers do. Many workers probably don't even realize how they terrify prospective parents. They've never been on the other side.

Joan walks into spotless homes knowing they've been cleaned for her benefit. She can sense the fears of working women who are afraid they'll be rejected because they are employed.

Some people have genuine impediments to adoption, which the home study is designed to uncover. These include:

- Arrests or a criminal conviction
- Serious mental or physical health problems
- Problems with drugs or alcohol abuse
- Unstable marriages
- A history of child abuse
- Lack of commitment to adopt

There also are problems that make some people ineligible for adoption through some agencies or from some countries (but not *all* agencies or countries). These include:

- Being single
- Being over a certain age (forty is a typical age barrier)
- Having biological children

If you fall into one of these categories, it doesn't mean you *can't* adopt. It just means you will have to search harder for an agency, or adopt from a country that will accept you.

You know yourself better than anyone else knows you. If you are a stable adult who is mentally, physically, and emotionally capable of nurturing children, that's what the social worker will be likely to see too. You may have a conflict with one social worker. Some, being human, rule out people they don't like, even if these people meet the general criteria. If you think this has happened to you, try another agency or another worker at the same agency.

You may think that you must be perfect to adopt a child, but you'll find very few saints or superparents among adoptive parents—just people who cared enough to submit to scrutiny to find the child of their dreams.

## SUMMARY

If your answers approximate those of successful adoptive parents, there's only one course to follow. Finish this book. Put aside your fears and get on with the process. You'll probably find that most of your fears were groundless.

The length and complexity of the adoption process is a hardship for most parents, but it has one major advantage. Parents have a long time to make this decision. They can back out at any stage.

Above all, if you desperately want to adopt, never give up hope.

CHAPTER 3

# Exploring Adoption Prospects

One of the hardest parts of any adoption is getting started. In this chapter we will help you explore adoption prospects in your community. We will discuss:

- Whom to contact
- Talking to families and agencies—what to ask and how to get through the barriers to obtain information
- How to evaluate your research

We suggest that you develop a time frame (such as one to three months) for your research, then close the process by evaluating your findings. You may decide you don't wish to go further. This is fine. At least you'll be making a decision.

## WHOM TO CONTACT

We suggest that you divide your research into two categories:

- Families that have adopted
- Licensed adoption agencies

You will need information from both families and agencies to develop a well-rounded picture of adoption. It may be easier to start with families who can, in turn, lead you to agencies. Adoption is like any other professional service. Your best referrals are usually by word of mouth.

## TALKING TO FAMILIES

Families that have adopted foreign children may be your best initial source of information. They can tell you how they adopted, offer information about agencies in your area, and answer many questions you might hesitate to ask a social worker. They can help you prepare for what a social worker might ask and ease your fears about the process. At one time, they probably felt many of those fears.

### Making Contact

If you don't know anyone who has adopted a foreign child, ask your relatives, friends, clergypersons, and others for suggestions. Some families love to help others explore adoption. Others feel it is an imposition. Ask your contact if the family is willing to talk before you call a complete stranger.

If you still can't locate anyone, check the Yellow Pages for Social Services. Then call United Way, the public library, the county or state social services department, or a large family counseling agency (e.g., Catholic Charities, Family Service, Lutheran Family Services) about groups of adoptive parents. Many cities have such organizations. There also are likely to be groups of intercultural families in larger communities. Officials of such groups often can suggest families that are willing to assist others.

Because adoption experiences differ widely, you should talk to more than one family. You'll begin to develop a realistic picture of adoption when you see that family styles, incomes, occupations, and child-rearing practices mirror the diversity of society. About equal numbers of blue- and white-collar families adopt. Seeing foreign adopted children in an American home is very helpful in visualizing what your family might be like.

### What to Ask

Here are some questions to ask the families you meet:

1. Where are the children from?
2. What agency did they work with?

3. How did they come to adopt?
4. What requirements did they have to meet?
5. What was their experience with their agency like?
6. What problems, if any, did they encounter?
7. How long did the adoption process take?
8. How much did it cost?
9. Did they have to travel abroad to pick up the child?
10. Can they recommend someone at their agency to call?
11. Will they call that person on your behalf?
12. What has their post-adoption experience with their children been?
13. What problems, if any, have they encountered as a foreign adoptive family?
14. How have the children adapted?
15. How well have the children been accepted by relatives and friends?
16. Did the children have any medical problems?
17. How have the children been accepted at school or by other children?
18. What have they done to help their children cope with adoption?
19. What tips would they offer a family starting a foreign adoption in their area?
20. If they had to do it over again, would they?

What you should get from talking to families is an introduction to the adoptive process and life as the parent of a foreign adopted child. Immediately after you leave, record your reactions.

- How did you feel about the experience?
- What impressed you about the experience?
- Did what they said cause you to feel that you couldn't adopt even though you still wanted to? If so, do you have the resources to overcome the perceived barrier?
- Did you feel that people who look different really can become a family?

These notes will be helpful when you evaluate your research.

## TALKING TO AGENCIES

Foreign adoption agencies by state are listed in chapter 20, but there may be additional licensed agencies in your area that provide such services. Check the sources that we suggested for locating families:

- The Yellow Pages of the nearest metropolitan phone book
- Churches, United Way, county and state social service departments
- The state adoption licensing agency or department
- The public library reference department

At this stage, explore the widest possible range of adoption options. You may have more choices than you would have imagined. You might fit a program that is open or you might need to broaden your search beyond the immediate area.

In this case, try the agencies throughout your state or region listed in chapter 20, or try to think of someone you know elsewhere who may have adopted internationally or have some access to foreign adoption. Start telling people you are interested in international adoption. They may make surprising but good suggestions. Eileen and Ron were led to Raj through a chance contact, though they did not initially use this approach. Joan found her adoption agency through Ray's mother, who had met an adoptive parent at a garage sale. There is an informal nationwide adoption network that is very effective if you actively seek contacts.

We stress the importance of searching for an agency. Do *not* try to do a private foreign adoption. Such adoptions are legally and financially dangerous. If you learn nothing else from this book, we hope you remember this point. There are numerous horror stories of innocent Americans desperate for a child who have given large sums of money to foreign lawyers and have ended up with neither money nor a child. There are tales of child selling and other abuses that endanger the continuation of legitimate foreign adoption programs. Periodically, nations have forbidden or severely curtailed foreign adoptions because of such scandals.

The safest thing to do is to search for a reputable agency that has access to children. These agencies may use private attorneys in foreign countries, but the attorneys have been screened. If you have any concerns about a program, call your county or state social services department or adoption licensing department.

*Don't even think about a private adoption. It won't work.*

## Getting Through to an Agency

Calling a list of adoption agencies is likely to give you some idea why persistence is one of the primary virtues adoptive families must have. It may be difficult. There are far more families interested in adoption than there are healthy infants, especially white infants. Many agencies have long waiting lists and discourage new applicants. This process starts with the way calls for information are handled.

Joan offers these tips for overcoming barriers to getting the information you need:

- Don't tell the receptionist you want information about adoption. Instead, say you are doing research on adoption and need the name of the person in charge.
- If you get the name, call later and ask for the individual by name.
- Be persistent. If the individual is out or busy, leave a message. If your call isn't returned within twenty-four hours, call again.
- If the individual is in the office but on another line, say you'll hold. Keep holding for at least five minutes.
- If you can't get through to the individual or a co-worker, ask if there is someone who can make an appointment for you.
- Be pleasant but don't give up. Eventually you'll find someone to talk to.
- Ask for printed information about the agency. Most agencies have a brochure that will provide answers to some questions.
- If possible, give the name of someone familiar to the social worker. This will help break the ice and give you credibility.
- If all else fails, put together and send the agency a small photo album (two to three pages) and some basic informa-

tion about yourself, your life-style, and why you want to adopt internationally. Ask the agency to call you. If they don't, call and ask if they received your album.

## What to Ask

When you make contact with a social worker, ask these questions (at least those relevant to your circumstances):

1. What types of children does your agency place?
2. What countries (including the U.S.) do your children come from?
3. Does your agency work locally or does it have access to national and international adoption networks?
4. How many children a year do you place?
5. What ages of children do you usually place?
6. Do you restrict acceptance of adoptive families on the basis of age, income, marital status, or religion? If so, what are the restrictions?
7. Will your agency work with single parents?
8. Will your agency work with divorced people (including those with prior marriages)?
9. Will your agency work with families that have biological children, children from a previous marriage, or other adopted children?
10. If you have been married only a short period of time but have been together longer, will the agency accept the longer length of time in its evaluation?
11. Does your agency offer an alternative program?
12. Does your agency offer information sessions for prospective parents?
13. How much does a typical domestic adoption cost?
14. How much does a typical foreign adoption cost?
15. What is the wait for a typical domestic adoption?
16. What is the wait for a typical foreign adoption?
17. What do you charge for your information session or other means of exploring adoption?
18. Does your agency do home studies and what is involved in a home study?
19. How much do you charge for a home study?

20. If we decide to go further, what is the next step and how do we take it?

## EVALUATING YOUR RESEARCH

After you've talked to one or two families and several agencies, compile and evaluate your results. Your goals should be:

• To decide if you want to explore further
• To narrow your search for an agency to one or two prospects

It is still too early for a final decision on adoption. It also is too early to commit more than token funds. You should, however, have begun to develop a sense of:

• Adoption prospects in your area
• The number of adoption options open to you
• Possible next steps

Your evaluation will be highly subjective. There are no clear-cut right or wrong answers.

### Evaluating Your Visits to Families

Think about how you felt when you visited the families. Review your notes. Ask yourself these questions:

• How did I feel when I saw the parents with their children? Was I scared? Awed? Attracted? Repelled?
• Could I imagine myself as the parent of such a child?
• How did I feel about the parents? Did I think they were lucky to have their children or did I think they were saints for having done something so noble?
• Do I want a child badly enough to spend a year or more filling out forms, waiting for the phone to ring, and battling the system?
• Even if I'm not sure yet that I'm capable of that, do I want to learn more?

27

- When I left, was I "up" and eager to do something similar or "down" and more frightened of the idea?

Be honest. If you still have lots of questions but are generally attracted to the idea, that's typical of this stage. If seeing families with foreign-born children made you uncomfortable, foreign adoption probably isn't for you.

## Evaluating Agencies

Review your notes and eliminate any agencies whose criteria you cannot meet. Then consider any comments from families. Add these to the notes you took on the agencies. They should weigh heavily in your final decision. It is especially important to note such things as whether families described various agencies as:

- Easy to work with
- Eager to place children
- Sensitive to the needs of parents

You will be spending a great deal of time with the agency you select. The relationship may be difficult because of the tensions built into the adoption process. If an agency consistently gets good reviews from parents, this is a very good sign. Consistent negative comments are a bad sign.

Assuming that you must choose between at least two agencies, ask yourself these questions:

1. Did anyone I talked to seem genuinely interested in helping me adopt? If so, this consideration should outweigh others. It is the key to a successful adoption experience.
2. Did the agency seem particularly bureaucratic or disinterested in me? Was it hard to get information? Bear in mind that some agencies can be difficult for prospective parents to work with before and during the approval process, but are warm and supportive after a child has been selected. Feedback from other parents is very useful on this point.
3. Did the agency request a large sum of money up front? At this stage, you should not be asked to pay more than a modest sum,

$200 or less, to attend an information session or be added to a waiting list. It is too soon to be asked to commit serious money.
4. Did the agency give me a feeling of hope that this might work? At this stage, *any* encouragement is a good sign that the agency is interested in helping you. Trust your instincts. Are these people you would feel comfortable working with on the most important "project" of your life for the next year or more?

When you've completed this initial assessment, turn to more practical questions and see how agencies compare:

- Does one agency offer a much broader range of children? The broader the range, the more options you have.
- Does one agency place much larger numbers of children? Don't eliminate small agencies. Just find out what your chances are of receiving one of a small number of children.
- Does one agency charge significantly more than the others? Find out more about what the charges include. The numbers may be misleading. Get a general breakdown before making any decision based on finances.
- Does one agency have a much longer wait than the others?
- Does one agency work with a country in which you are especially interested?

You may want to obtain more details about the number of children placed by your agencies from each country. However, even very small programs can result in the placements you most want. This was Eileen's experience twice.

Add it all up. You'll probably see a pattern that will suggest your next step.

If the agencies seem about equal and you haven't met any parents who have adopted through any of them (or you have parental feedback on one and not the others) ask the agencies for names of families. If the agencies won't provide such names (for privacy reasons), ask someone in an adoptive parent group or intercultural family organization for suggestions.

When you've selected an agency, call for an appointment or register for the next adoption information session. One final note. If possible, work through an agency that has an office reasonably close to you. Your regional agency knows what your state requires for adoption. It will handle all matters requiring state approval. This is a tremendous advantage.

Not only are state requirements difficult to understand, state adoption workers aren't sure what to do with unusual papers or prospective parents who don't fit their system.

When Eileen was adopting Raj, she spent an entire morning trying to get a piece of paper moved from one desk in the State Welfare Department to another because the worker wasn't sure Mother Teresa's program met Nebraska requirements. Since Mother Teresa's American representative lived in Washington, D.C., it was up to Eileen to persuade Nebraska authorities. She finally called the department's assistant director, who took care of the matter for her. If she hadn't known this man (whom she met when she was a newspaper reporter), she would have had to take a day of vacation to accomplish the mission.

Joan spent hours trying to get someone in the Department of Social Services to find the home study for her first adoption. It had been misfiled under a similar name. A good regional agency will fight these battles for you or you can avoid them entirely.

But if you cannot qualify for any of your local agencies or you are not satisfied with them and you still want to do a foreign adoption, extend your search. Your road will be harder, but many people have traveled such roads successfully—including both authors.

## QUESTIONS AND COMMENTS TO AVOID

Here are some questions and comments to avoid:

1. Did you adopt because you couldn't have children? (As Ann Landers would say, mind your own business.)
2. What do you know about the *real* parents? (Adoptive parents *are* real parents, just not birth parents. Start getting used to the terminology.)
3. Does it bother you that your child's skin is dark? (Good adoptive parents love their children the way God made them. They don't want their gorgeous dark-skinned Indian son to resemble his blue-eyed blonde mother.)

30

4. How smart will the child be? (Adoptive kids come in a full range of IQs just like birth kids.)
5. We think it's time Johnny had a playmate. (Adopted children are not pets or toys.)
6. (When you're adopting a baby) Will the child speak English? (Is this the language you plan to use in your home?)
7. (Infant adoption from Asia) The child must love rice. (Certainly, and whatever else you feed him.)

Even if you make a mistake or ask an adoptive parent a question that seems stupid, don't worry about it. Experienced adoptive parents are old hands at this. They might have even asked a few silly questions themselves when they were just starting out.

CHAPTER 4

# How Is Foreign Adoption Different?

It was a typical Saturday outing. Eileen and the children had gone to the zoo, then stopped for ice cream. The children chattered happily, but Eileen was distracted. She noticed that a large man in a nearby booth seemed to be taking an inordinate interest in them.

Blowing cigarette smoke in her face, he approached and asked loudly, "Did you adopt them? Where they from? I think it's wonderful for you people to do something like this."

Raj fell silent. Shanti's face froze. She refused even to look at the man.

Eileen tried to politely extricate her family from this intrusion. "We adopted Raj from India and Shanti from Thailand, but we were as lucky as they are.

"Come on, kids. It's time to get going."

Pointedly, Eileen and the children gathered their things and left the ice-cream shop. Eileen suspected that the man had no idea that he had ruined a pleasant afternoon.

If the children had been white, no one would have suspected that they were adopted, and it would have been unthinkable for someone to barge up and comment on it. Such is life in a foreign adopted family.

In this chapter we will explore the differences between foreign and domestic adoption. These differences may be broken into two major categories:

- Emotional and cultural
- Practical and procedural

## EMOTIONAL AND CULTURAL DIFFERENCES

Joan says she sometimes believes that the only similarities between foreign and domestic adoption are that both use the word *adoption* and involve the placement of a child in a family. Even before a child arrives, foreign adoptive families face cultural and emotional questions that don't arise in domestic adoptions. They must accept the fact that even complete strangers will feel free to comment on matters that normally would be private. Parents need to look deeply into themselves and, in some cases, accept the need to change and grow. This can be exciting, but is also painful and difficult. Some of the major issues that prospective parents must confront include:

• Their feelings about people of other races and cultures
• Their close relatives' feelings about people of other races and cultures
• Their ability to cope with overt and covert bigotry in society
• Their willingness to incorporate another culture in their family
• Their ability to cope with being "on display"

Most people need to explore these issues with an experienced social worker. Do not be discouraged if you are frightened, ambivalent, or unsure about what you think or feel or how you might cope. These will be among the most difficult issues you face, and most people gradually grow more comfortable with them as they move through the adoption process. Some people see Eastern European adoptions as a way to escape these problems because the children are white. However, this is only partially true. The cultural and adoptive issues still must be addressed.

### 1. Feelings About People of Other Races and Cultures

No one grows up completely unbiased against or comfortable with people who are different from themselves. This becomes very important when foreign adoption is being considered. While our society no longer condones expressions of bigotry, prospective adoptive parents must examine what, if any, biases they have. This can be very painful. While you probably will need to work through this critical question with the help of a trained counselor, you can start by thinking about your experiences with people of other races and cultures and how you responded to them. Some questions you might ask yourself include:

- Have I ever spent any time with people of other backgrounds?
- Have I ever had a close friend of a different background?
- Have I ever been the only person of my race or background at a gathering? How did I react?
- What do I remember my parents or other relatives saying about different racial and cultural groups? (Even though you may have rejected blatant biases, those messages are still part of your conditioning and you need to think about what effect they had on you. You may have to sensitize your extended family.)
- Do I subconsciously believe that my racial/ethnic/religious group is superior to others?
- Do I feel some groups are inferior? If so, which ones?
- Do I feel especially uncomfortable with any cultures that I know about? If so, which ones?

It is easier to answer such questions if you have known people of different backgrounds and especially if you have friends of different backgrounds. It is not necessary to feel equally comfortable with all racial and ethnic groups. At this stage it is important to admit to yourself if you have any biases that you can identify. It also is important to begin learning more about your reactions to people different from yourself if you simply have no experience with other groups.

One of the better ways to do this is to get involved with international groups such as foreign-student host-family programs, Rotary International exchange programs, foreign-tourist "home stay" programs, and so on. Call your United Way, public library, Chamber of Commerce, a local university, or city or county tourism office for more information about opportunities in your area.

## 2. Relatives' Feelings About People of Different Races

No matter how unbiased you are, you must examine the feelings of your relatives toward people of other backgrounds. If you adopt, your child will become part of your total family and will have to cope with any biases of his/her grandparents and other relatives. Think about your relatives, especially your parents.

- What types of things have you heard them say about people of other races and backgrounds?
- If you ever brought home a friend of a different background, how did they react?
- Do you think they could accept a child who is "different" as a full member of the family? For that matter, could they accept *any* adopted child as a full member of the family?
- Do you have any relatives who are important to you who have strong biases?
- If your relatives are biased, how important is this likely to be in your child's day-to-day life? (If you see your parents once a year, it's less important than if your mother lives down the block and visits every day.)
- How open to change do you think your relatives might be?

This last question is critical. We have seen many families open their hearts to adopted children even if they were initially unsure about the idea. While it is difficult to predict, some family patterns may give clues:

- Have the parents accepted other things which they initially opposed in the interests of family harmony? (For example, how have they adjusted when a child has married someone of another religion or race or has been divorced?)
- Would your parents risk losing contact with one of their children over a major issue or would they feel that "keeping" their children is the top priority?
- Are your parents warm people who relate well to children? (It's hard for someone who likes children to resist a foreign-born grandchild for long.)
- Are your parents terribly concerned about what others may think? (It could be difficult if they would regard the new grandchild as a social embarrassment and place concern for what their friends might think ahead of love for the child.)

## 3. Coping with Society's Bigotry

Even if you and your relatives are totally unbiased, you must face the fact that you will raise a minority child in a society that is still afflicted with racial bias. If you are white, your child will face problems that you've never had to cope with. He or she will be "different" from many of his or her classmates and relatives. Your child will get questions from other children that will be painful for you. You will be very vulnerable to the hurts that your child suffers. You will want to protect your child and find that you can't.

Yet it would be a mistake to get too concerned at this point about how you will handle social bigotry, because you and your child may encounter very little of it. Mixed race families of all types are more common than they were a generation ago. There are more intermarriages and foreign adoptions. There are more single parents and "blended families" and other variations on the traditional family. The nation's Asian and Hispanic populations are growing rapidly. It is likely that your child will have classmates who are Asian and Hispanic. At this stage, you should think about questions such as:

- Am I terribly concerned about what other people think?
- Have I ever taken an independent stand on something? Would I ever do something like this again?
- Does it bother me if someone criticizes me, even if I know the criticism is unfair or unjust?
- Have I ever spoken out against bigotry or challenged a racist or sexist remark?
- If I've ever spent time with a person of another race, have I felt people were staring at us or worried what strangers might think?
- In general, am I a bit of a risk taker?

If you are willing to take an independent stand, you're much more likely to handle any problems with bigotry better than someone who worries a lot about what others think. While white American society has probably never been more open to foreign adoption than it is now, it is still "different" and you will encounter occasional strange reactions from some people. Most

successful foreign adoptive parents learn to pay very little attention to those reactions. They tend to feel that the other person has
a problem.

## 4. Incorporating Another Culture

Americans who adopt foreign-born children change the racial
and ethnic character of their families forever. What happens can
best be expressed in two paradoxes:

- Adopted foreign children retain their birth identities while
becoming very American.
- Adoptive families need to incorporate their child's birth heritage into the family, while striving to avoid making the child
feel "different."

These may sound mutually exclusive. It is not surprising that
experienced adoptive parents constantly work to discover and
maintain the right balance between the birth and American heritages and cultures. There is no single correct solution. Most families manage to work out something that feels comfortable for
them. See the suggestions in chapter 9 for ways of doing this.

Above all, parents must accept their children for what they are.
If your child senses that you'd really prefer him or her to be white
instead of Oriental or Latin American, you're headed for trouble.
That's why you must look so searchingly at your attitudes toward
other people.

## 5. Life on Display

When you adopt a foreign child, it's no secret from anyone.
This may or may not bother you. Most foreign adoptive parents
find that their children get more than the usual public attention
given to children. If you have a friendly, cute baby or toddler,
people will notice and talk to either you or the child. Clerks in
stores are more likely to remember you and your child.

This can be fun if both you and your child are outgoing. Raj was
an eye-catching baby who would smile at anyone. Early on, he
learned that he could get extra cookies or suckers at grocery
stores. He seemed to thrive on the attention. Shanti, by contrast,

hated it. She froze when strangers told her how cute she was. She loathed being touched.

If you are shy, you may be unable to cope with the spotlight. Even outgoing parents may find certain aspects of life on display distasteful:

- Having strangers ask you loudly in front of your children (who, of course, are deaf, dumb, and insensitive): "Who's their *real* mother?"
- Having strangers ask you loudly in front of your children: "What language do they speak?" (Of course your children don't understand English and couldn't possibly understand this ridiculous question. What language does your interrogator imagine *you* speak to your children—Korean?)
- Having well-meaning people commend you for your nobility in front of the children. (This tends to make your kids feel like refugees from a CARE poster and puts you in the awkward position of trying to correct someone who meant no harm.)
- Having strangers (or even friends) ask if you adopted the children because you couldn't have any. (Surely adoptive parents are entitled to privacy about very personal medical problems, if that's the case.)
- Never knowing when your privacy will be breached. (Eventually you get used to it, but it can be unsettling.)

Compensations include the ability to occasionally help someone who wants to adopt, the ability to combat stereotypes about adoption, and the opportunity to meet new friends.

## PRACTICAL AND PROCEDURAL DIFFERENCES

Adopting a foreign child is both easier and harder than adopting an American child.
- It is easier because there are children available for adoption and the wait is usually shorter.
- It is harder because the paperwork is far more complex and more players are involved.

Procedures and requirements vary from agency to agency and from country to country. However, in general, in a domestic adoption, you must get a home study, locate a child, then file for adoption in a local court. In a foreign adoption, typically you must:

- Locate an agency that works in foreign adoption and fill out an application.
- Have a home study done.
- When a child is located, fill out whatever forms the court in that country requires. Copies of your birth certificate, marriage license, income and employment records, health and possibly psychological certificates and police records usually are needed in triplicate, notarized and accompanied by certificates authenticating the notary. You also may have to pay a translation fee.
- File for U.S. Immigration Service permission for the child to enter this country.
- Travel to the country (in some cases). Some countries require two trips.
- File for local adoption.
- Have the child naturalized.

Most agencies provide detailed instructions on filling out the required foreign court forms. The chart on page 105 gives information about what various countries require.

Even though the requirements sound complicated, the support that becomes available to families once a child is identified compensates for any difficulty. Agency workers become almost as eager as adoptive parents to bring the children home.

## SUMMARY

The mental preparation for a foreign adoption is extremely important. It can be exciting, challenging, and rewarding. Once you get a child, you may wonder what the big deal was. When you can look at your beautiful Asian or Latin American son or daughter and simply see a child whom you love passionately, you know that you've worked through all the steps. From time to time, you may continue to be bothered by the insensitivity of others—more from your child's standpoint than your own—but successful foreign-adoptive parents regard such incidents as a small price to pay for the joy of having their children.

The extensive paperwork connected with foreign adoption may be viewed in somewhat the same light. Once you have completed it, you may look back in astonishment at what you've had to do, but you will mercifully forget most of it pretty soon. Your child will be more than worth it.

CHAPTER 5

# Can We Afford This Venture?

When most Americans buy a home or a college education for their children, they don't plan to pay the full amount up front. Even conservative spenders know that these major investments can safely be paid off over a period of time. They're more concerned about getting good value for their money than saving a few dollars here and there.

We believe that this is a good way to think about financing a foreign adoption. Sure it's a major expense, but what better investment could you make? And, like a home, you can pay for an adoption over a period of time if money is a problem. In this chapter, we will discuss:

- Total adoption costs
- What you should expect to pay for various services
- Variation in costs by country
- Creative ways of financing adoption costs

## TOTAL COSTS

A typical foreign adoption will cost you from $5,000 to $16,000. Costs vary considerably by country and by agency. Some agencies charge flat fees for services. Others use a sliding scale depending on a family's income. There are numerous variations. Some agencies offer special assistance to families adopting children with special needs. There are no government subsidies for international adoptions as there are for some domestic adoptions.

In trying to determine how much a foreign adoption will cost, remember that many agency estimates include only their own fees. They may not include miscellaneous expenses, which can add up. Be sure to ask your agency precisely what is and is not covered. Some additional expenses include:

- Photocopying and postage
- Fees to local and state government agencies for certified, notarized, and authenticated copies of documents
- Long-distance phone calls
- Travel to foreign countries or within the United States

## Agency Fees

In exploring adoption options, you may be tempted to select a program simply because it charges less. This is unwise. We urge you to pick the agency whose program appeals to you most strongly and assume that you will find a way to pay the costs.

If two agencies seem otherwise equal, select the one with lower fees, but double check what those fees cover. If an agency's costs are dramatically higher than its competitors, try to find out why. If the agency can't justify its fees, go elsewhere. You probably wouldn't have a good relationship with such an agency anyway.

Remember that social agencies know many parents who can and will pay whatever they ask without too many questions. Some agencies use adoption fees to assist the orphanages from which the children come. Other hidden costs that your fees underwrite include: administration or program fees such as trips abroad for agency personnel to locate children for adoption, staff time, and international communications (long-distance phone calls, overseas postage, and courier services).

No reputable agency will exploit the great demand for children by charging exorbitant fees and making a profit. However, some may not offer flexible financing because no one has ever asked. Ask about options. If you genuinely cannot afford what an agency charges as opposed to being unwilling to pay the fees, some of the suggestions later in this chapter might work for you.

## Miscellaneous Costs

Be sure to budget several hundred dollars for miscellaneous costs such as payments for documents, photocopying, and postage. These add up much faster than you might think, especially since documents usually need to be in triplicate, are voluminous and must be sent overseas by courier. In addition, you will be making a number of long-distance phone calls connected with the adoption, possibly even some international calls.

## COSTS BY COUNTRY

Costs differ dramatically from country to country. The list of countries on pages 104-7 gives approximate estimates that you might expect to pay for adoptions from various nations as this book goes to print in 1993. Remember, our numbers are only estimates. Individual circumstances might affect your costs. Inflation also might affect costs. However, unless something major changes (new regulations, new restrictions, and so on) the relative ranking of countries should remain the same.

Because airfares differ dramatically from time to time and place to place, we have not attempted to include these costs in our chart, but we have noted the countries that require trips, the number of trips currently required, and the average length of stay required. Ask a good travel agent what such a trip might cost, including estimated daily food and lodging costs.

Check out budget travel books from your public library for names of nice but reasonable hotels. In addition, ask if your agency knows of a guest house where you can stay for below average rates. If you must stay for an extended period, a "bed and breakfast" arrangement in a private home might be preferable to a hotel. Ask foreign students or natives of the country you'll be visiting and your agency for names of possible host families.

If you have a major credit card, you can pay for both airfare and overseas hotel bills with "plastic." Both VISA and MasterCard allow you to spread the expense out over a longer period of time; VISA, MasterCard, and American Express are among the credit cards widely accepted around the world. (You can also purchase souvenirs with your charge card even in off-the-beaten-track locations.)

# CREATIVE WAYS TO FINANCE ADOPTION*

*(Information in this section of the chapter is based heavily on "Financing an Adoption" by Jerri Ann Jenista, which appeared in *OURS Magazine*, November/December 1990.)

If you genuinely cannot afford an agency's adoption charges, discuss the situation with your social worker. Agencies are accustomed to dealing with clients for whom finances are a problem.

Do not be put off by agencies that tell you that if you cannot afford the adoption fees, you probably cannot afford the child. Anyone from a big family knows that there's always room for one more if hearts are generous. On the other hand, many families would be pressed to come up with a large sum of cash at one time. It's the difference between saving the down payment on your home (which seems to take years) and making the monthly payment. Don't apologize if you fall into the "monthly payment" category.

One of your first major expenditures is the home study, which can cost from $1,000 to $3,000. If you don't have that kind of ready money, consider these alternatives:

- Will your agency allow you to make monthly payments over a period of time? Some agencies permit you to pay a portion at the beginning, another portion later, and the final installment when the study is complete. If this schedule is too ambitious for you, see if you can spread your payments over six months or even a year.
- Will your agency allow you to swap services for some or all of your fee? Be creative. Are you an artist or a writer? You might design a brochure. Can you do office work or bookkeeping or other jobs needed by the agency? Many agencies have difficulty keeping some positions filled because of their low pay scales. See what you can arrange.
- Ask your church or local philanthropies for help. This may be difficult for you, but remember, they are being asked to help a child, not you. This is especially true if you are adopting a child with special needs from a country with which the group already has a relationship. Maybe your church or some other group would hold a benefit for a fund established

for your child with a social service agency. Agencies usually can supply promotional materials for such events.

• Your relatives may be willing to lend you money at little or no interest. You might also borrow money from your friends. Be careful. You can permanently ruin relationships if you fail to repay the money. Reduce the chances of this by writing out the terms of the loan with copies to both parties.

• Finance companies, credit unions, and banks may be willing to lend money for adoption. Consider asking for a "home-improvement loan" that carries a lower interest rate.

• Consider borrowing money against your life-insurance policies. These often have extremely low interest rates of 2 percent to 5 percent. You also can borrow against the equity in your home.

• Ask your agency if it has a "scholarship" or loan fund, especially if you are adopting a child with special needs.

• If you're having trouble paying foreign court fees "up front," ask if your agency will accept payments over a period of time. This may not be possible at a very small agency, or even a large agency, but it never hurts to ask.

• If your child has an unusual medical or genetic condition, see if an international or national foundation will help. While very few such groups would help subsidize an adoption, they could offer you useful information, support families, and notice of free drug or treatment trials. When your child arrives, contact the local affiliate of the national foundation for your child's condition to see what help it can provide. You may be amazed to discover how many health foundations and self-help groups there are and what a range of problems they cover. There is a nonrecurring federal subsidy to cover adoption expenses for children with special needs. To receive up to $1,500 for such an adoption, apply to your state department of social services before you finalize your adoption. You will receive the funds after finalization.

In addition:

• You may be eligible for a state tax deduction or some other benefits.

45

- Some military and civil service families may apply for reimbursement of certain adoption expenses.
- Some major corporations offer benefit plans in which employees can select from a "menu" of choices. Is adoption a possibility? What about paid time off?
- If your company allows time off for adoption, ask about using some of that time for a trip abroad if one is required. If two trips are required, you may be able to split your adoption leave or vacation to meet this demand. You may be able to negotiate for extended days without pay or schedule travel over a regular long weekend.
- Explore options for reducing the cost of travel, such as escorting medical supplies or documents on your outbound trip in return for a lower fee.
- Ask your agency if it can make travel arrangements for lower than normal fares. Some agencies buy blocks of tickets.
- Becoming a host family for a student from the country to which you will be traveling could pay large dividends on your trip. You may be invited to spend a night or two or have dinner with your student's parents. They might be able to interpret or show you around.

Eileen and Ron marvel at the hospitality they have received in numerous countries. Relatives of student friends have picked them up at airports in the middle of the night, driven them all over remote cities, thrown parties in their honor, and forbidden them to purchase even a soda.

## POSTPLACEMENT FEES

Read your medical and dental insurance plans carefully to ensure that you and your child receive all benefits to which you are entitled. You may be asked to produce some official statement that you have legal custody before your coverage includes your new child. You will probably have to wait until your child arrives to add him or her to your policy. Make this your top priority the day after your child comes home.

If you face expenses, such as immunization of your family for hepatitis, try to persuade your insurance company to cover the cost even if they argue that it is not a "routine immunization." Remind your employee benefits representative or insurance agent that prevention is much cheaper than care for even one family member who falls seriously ill.

Use the negotiating and advocacy skills you have mastered during the course of your adoption to obtain appropriate assistance for your new child, even if it means battling several layers of bureaucracy and several turn-downs. If what you request is reasonable, you should win, especially if what you want for your child is less expensive than an item (such as a wheelchair) that would normally be covered.

## THE LILIES OF THE FIELD

Most people adopting children assume that they will pay the costs of rearing them, just as they would biological children. However, there are some special parents who adopt children who might otherwise grow up in orphanages or other institutions. Many of these families have large hearts and small budgets. In some semimiraculous fashion, others are inspired by their generosity and quietly help out.

One of Eileen's friends is close to such a family. When she makes a casserole or lasagna, she sometimes prepares extra and gives it to her friends. People like these don't worry too much about the usual financial questions that trouble most adoptive families, especially first-time parents. They seem to take the biblical illustration of the lilies of the field to heart (the verse in which Christ reminds us not to worry too much about money but to "consider the lilies of the field, how they grow; they neither toil nor spin, yet I tell you, even Solomon in all his glory was not clothed like one of these" [Matthew 6:28, 29]) and somehow it seems to work.

We aren't advocating that you take this approach to your finances, but there are valuable lessons in it. Children can grow up much better in homes with abundant love and limited money than the contrary. Children in such families learn to share and save. They learn at a young age that spending-money is earned, not given, and they learn to look out for others. Those aren't bad lessons for young people to absorb.

## SUMMARY

We believe that people who want to adopt badly enough can and will find the money to do so. Our final recommendations for coping with the financial burdens of adoption include:

- Start saving a given amount a month as soon as you begin to seriously consider adoption. You'll be surprised how it mounts up. Eileen financed a major portion of Raj's adoption through renting a room to a foreign student. She began putting this money in a special savings account as soon as she made contact with Mother Teresa's representative. By the time Raj arrived, she had painlessly collected most of the funds she needed.
- If need be, swallow your pride and ask others to help.
- Ask other parents in your area who have adopted if they know of any sources of help, especially if you are adopting a child with special needs.
- Be realistic about the costs of adopting from different countries. If you don't care terribly which country your child comes from (assuming that you qualify for several countries) pick one within your means. But don't rule out a trip abroad because of the expense. Remember that adoption is an investment.
- Travel to get your child is an investment in understanding your child. Such understanding may pay a lifetime of "dividends." Even if two or three trips are required, they probably will be worth the money.
- Start early in exploring your company's adoption leave and medical-insurance policies. If you think changes need to be made, request a meeting with employee benefits representatives. At a minimum, you may plant a seed that could result in improvements for future adoptive families. This might even include you on a later adoption.
- Finally, at the risk of sounding naive, remember the lilies of the field. Part of the miracle of adoption is that somehow it usually works out.

CHAPTER 6

# Getting Started

You've decided to cope with the special challenges and joys of a foreign adoption. Your next step is unavoidable: the Home Study.

Home studies are required for all adoptions and they follow a fairly uniform format. In addition to filling out an application giving basic family information, you will be required to submit to individual and joint interviews (if you are married) and a home visit. You will be asked for original copies of your birth and marriage certificates (if you are married). These can be obtained from the Bureau of Vital Statistics in the states where you were born and married. Generally these offices are in the state capitals. Call first to check on charges and the exact information you must supply to obtain the documents. Order at least three of each. You'll need them sooner or later.

You also will be asked to supply documentation about your income, employment, and health, and provide letters of recommendation. Some agencies specify who must write these letters (e.g., clergy, employer, or doctor). Others allow the prospective parents to select the authors. You probably will have to submit to police and child-protective checks. Some agencies require psychological tests such as the MMPI (Minnesota Multiphasic Personality Inventory). Most people are nervous about their home studies. Like final exams, the specter is usually worse than the experience.

We offer one word of caution. Some agencies offer "generic" home studies for what may sound like bargain prices. These are home studies unconnected with a specific foreign program or child. Be careful. Having such a study done may turn out to be a waste of time and money. Nearly all agencies that place children insist on doing their own or having them done by a social worker whom they have approved in advance. Do not even think of having a home study done until you have cleared all arrangements with the agency that will be placing your child.

## SELECTING A COUNTRY

During your workshops and home study, you and your social worker will probably discuss the nationality of the child you want to adopt. Your final selection will probably be determined by such practical considerations as:

- The countries your agency works with
- The countries you qualify for
- The countries that are "open" at the moment
- What age child you want
- How long you are willing to wait
- Whether you are willing to travel to the country and, if so, how many trips you are willing to make and how long you can stay
- Costs

Many families have strong preferences as to age and sex and much weaker preferences about countries. Many are delighted to accept a child from any country that will most quickly give them a child of the desired age and sex. Chapter 19 includes brief descriptions of the countries from which many foreign adopted children come to the United States. This may help you begin thinking of options.

Your social worker will help you work through possibilities and might recommend applying for more than one country. Strong preferences for particular countries add to the difficulty of adoption. But you might not mind a longer wait or doing more paperwork if you have close ties to particular countries, as Ron and Eileen did to both India and Thailand.

Selecting a country is usually one of the easiest parts of foreign adoption. It becomes more difficult when you must settle down to wait for a referral from the country you have chosen.

# WAITING

Most agencies maintain waiting lists by country. Typically you will be told that your name is on the list of the country you have chosen and that you probably will hear something in a given number of months. This usually is an educated guess.

Events are now completely out of your hands. Your agency will be trying to match your application with the dossiers of available children provided by its foreign adoption counterparts. At most, you may receive a few hints as to what is happening.

After the intensity of the home study and the excitement of choosing a country, a sense of letdown and even mild depression are not unusual. It may be hard to believe that the adoption will ever take place, especially if you've been told to expect a wait of six months or more. Some people feel that they are moving further away from adoption rather than coming closer to it.

Consider this wait as a sort of "adoptive pregnancy." You can use the time very productively to prepare for your new arrival. Even though you won't experience the physical changes of pregnancy, you need the interlude to get ready. To make the months pass faster and to keep the adoption real in your mind, we suggest that you devote spare hours to becoming acquainted with the nation from which your child will come.

Check out books at the library. Sample the cuisine at local restaurants (if available). Contact a local college or university to see if there are any students from your child's country. Most would be pleased to meet an American family, especially when they learn of your adoption plans. You may want to learn a bit of your child's birth language, especially if you are adopting an older child. Check your local library for books and tapes.

This also is an excellent period for spoiling yourself just a bit. It will be many years before you again have as much time and money, and it may help you maintain your morale. Do the things that will be difficult when you have a child. Try the restaurants you've read about. Go to the movies you've been meaning to see. Splurge on a weekend away from home.

If you aren't into a fitness routine, this is an excellent time to start. Regular exercise does wonders for your mental and physical

51

health. It will increase your energy, and you'll need all the energy you can get when your child comes.

These months are an important part of your preparation for parenthood. Although you probably will go about your daily life much as you did before, nothing will be quite the same. Like your pregnant friends, you're expecting a child!

## TELLING PEOPLE

When should you tell people about your adoption plans? A lot depends on your personality. Some prospective parents tell everyone they know as soon as they decide to adopt, before they even select an agency. Others tell only their closest relatives and friends until a child is assigned.

The greatest drawback to telling everyone that you are planning to adopt is that you will be questioned endlessly during this waiting period about matters over which you have no control. This may make the wait even more difficult, especially if it is prolonged. It can cause embarrassment and added pain if you are rejected.

On the other hand, an announcement that you have applied for adoption puts an end to the "why don't you people get with it and have a kid" questions to which so many childless couples are subjected. Choosing to tell some relatives and friends but not others can hurt feelings. If you choose to tell only a handful of people, be sure they can keep your secret.

Any way you do it, sharing news of the planned adoption with special people is one of the joys of the process. You may be surprised to learn just how much pleasure your announcement gives other people. You also may be surprised to discover how many other families have adopted and what a bond this creates.

## WE HAVE A CHILD FOR YOU!

Finally *the* day you've waited for arrives, often when you least expect it. It's a never-to-be-forgotten moment: that call at work or that message on your answering machine when you've just come back from the grocery store. Almost any adoptive parent can tell you exactly what he or she was doing when the call came and how he or she reacted to it.

"I think we've got a child for you. When can you come take a look at the picture?" Or "How soon can you finish your paperwork and travel to meet your child?"

There's an almost unbelievable electricity in those words. There's a child for me! This is real! We're going to be parents! The months of waiting seem to vanish and God may seem very close. You may find yourself both laughing and crying before you even see the picture—or doing both at the same time! It may be hard to resist dashing to the car as you hang up the phone.

In the notification phone call, your social worker will give you critical information about age, sex, nationality, and health. Then you select the first available moment to collect one of the most precious bits of paper you will ever receive—your first photo of your child.

Adoption pictures are notoriously awful. They tend to resemble prison mug shots. No sane prospective parent would reject a child because he or she doesn't look handsome/beautiful in the photo. No matter how dreadful the photo is, the child will look beautiful to you. When you actually meet your child, you may wonder how such a gorgeous child could have taken such a horrible photo.

Available referral information can be extremely sketchy or quite detailed, depending on the agency and the country. The questions that might most concern you—family health history and intelligence—are seldom answered. If you are adopting a child with special needs, you should get some information about the handicaps.

In most cases, acceptance of a referral that meets the requested age, sex, and health criteria is all but a foregone conclusion. Valid reasons for refusing a referral include the child's not meeting one of the parents' original specifications. In such cases, the agencies need a prompt response so they can locate other parents.

If you instantly fall in love with the picture and accept the child, you're ready to tackle one of the hardest parts of the adoption process.

## FINAL PAPERWORK

Until now, you've only been playing at adoption paperwork. Along with your child's picture, you will receive instructions as to what papers and forms must be filed with the foreign government to complete the adoption. Depending on the country, these can be voluminous. At a minimum you will once again be asked to produce certified copies of your birth and marriage certificates. (Here's where you use the extra copies you ordered during the home study.)

You may feel like you're plowing very familiar turf as you fill out more application forms, once more provide verification of health and income and submit still more letters of recommendation. You may need to be fingerprinted for a police check (if you haven't already had to do this to have a child assigned). You also will need to have everything notarized and obtain certificates authenticating the notaries. These certificates can be obtained from your Secretary of State's office and must be dated *after* the documents were notarized. The notary stamp should not expire for at least a year. The papers may not be seen in the foreign country for a year. There is usually a charge for each certificate of authenticity, so use one notary for all documents.

After months of waiting, you will be under tremendous pressure to complete your dossier as quickly as possible. Now, however, you have a great incentive. Every day you delay is one more day before your child arrives.

Different countries require different procedures for dossiers. In some cases, documents will have to be translated. In others, materials will have to be approved by the consulate of your child's country and/or the U.S. State Department. Your social worker will provide detailed instructions and guide you through some of the more difficult bureaucratic procedures.

## IMMIGRATION PAPERWORK

You also will need to obtain permission from the U.S. Immigration and Naturalization Service (INS) to bring your child into this country. This is routine if you have obtained your referral from a licensed American adoption agency. It can be extremely difficult if you have not.

We will not try to explain the complexities of U.S. immigration rules governing foreign adoption because licensed U.S. agencies handle most of those matters for parents. They will only place children who qualify as "orphans" under American immigration standards. Some Americans have gone to Romania (and elsewhere) only to find that their adopted child has been refused an

I-600A visa to enter the U.S. because the child does not meet immigration criteria.

If you are adopting through an agency, do not worry. Compliance with immigration rules is a major reason we strongly urge you to adopt only through a licensed agency. You can obtain the I-600A Form from your nearest INS office. The INS workers will give you detailed instructions. You can even file for a visa before your child is identified, then complete your application after you receive a referral. You will need to supply INS with proof of your U.S. citizenship, proof of marriage (if married), proof of the termination of any prior marriages (if applicable), a favorable recommendation on your home study, and fingerprint cards.

District INS offices are located in the following cities: Anchorage; Atlanta; Baltimore; Boston; Buffalo; Chicago; Cleveland; Dallas; Denver; Detroit; El Paso; Harlingen, Texas; Hartford; Helena; Honolulu; Houston; Kansas City, Missouri; Los Angeles; Miami; Newark; New Orleans; New York; Omaha; Philadelphia; Phoenix; Portland, Maine; Portland, Oregon; St. Paul; San Antonio; San Diego; San Francisco; Seattle; and Washington, D.C.

There also are INS offices in: Albany; Albuquerque; Charleston, South Carolina; Charlotte, North Carolina; Cincinnati; Fresno, California; Indianapolis; Jacksonville; Las Vegas; Louisville; Memphis; Merrillville, Indiana; Milwaukee; Norfolk, Virginia; Oklahoma City; Pittsburgh; Providence; Reno; St. Albans, Vermont; St. Louis; Salt Lake City; San Jose; Spokane; Tampa; and Tucson.

If you go abroad to bring back your child, you will complete immigration processing at the U.S. Embassy or Consulate in your child's country. Your adoption agency will provide you with detailed instructions.

Once you have filed your I-600A, it's time to wait until you are notified either that you can go to pick up your child or that your child will be arriving.

## MORE WAITING

This time, the waiting will have a feel entirely different from before. You now have a picture to show the world. A CHILD IS COMING!

Ironically, now that you are waiting for *your* child, it may be even harder. You may find yourself worrying about his health or wondering what she's doing. You may feel that every day of waiting is a day stolen from your life together. Some agencies supply periodic updates on children, complete with pictures. These can be reassuring, but they also tend to make parents impatient for the day of arrival.

Now you can really begin to get ready for your child. You can decorate the room, look for child care, or get acquainted with schools in your area. You may want to join an intercultural-families group if you haven't already done so. Others who have already experienced what you're going through may be more understanding than lifelong friends.

You may find your relationship with your agency growing closer and warmer. Your case will now be a top agency priority—an enormous improvement over the months when you were just another name on a waiting list. The agency is as eager as you are to bring your child home. Your calls will be returned promptly and your problems addressed with dispatch.

Unexpected difficulties may still arise (as Eileen found in Shanti's adoption—see chapter 17). But even in these cases, there's a difference. The agency has invested a lot in helping you succeed. It should help you over any remaining hurdles.

## BRINGING YOUR CHILD HOME

At length, you will be notified of a specific date when you can either pick up your child in the United States or go to the foreign country to complete processing. With countries that require two trips, you will be given a date for a preliminary hearing or procedure with final placement after your second trip.

If your child is being flown to the U.S., you may have to go to another city to meet him or her. You also will have to pay airfare and/or an escort fee. Some agencies will arrange for your child to come directly to your city or to the nearest large community, but this is unusual. Plan on a trip to a "hub" airport unless you are extraordinarily lucky. Your agency may ask you to supply clothes and toys for the flight to the United States. They will give specific instructions.

It may be wise to plan an overnight stay in the hub city. Your child will be exhausted after the long international flight. He will have his nights and days mixed up and be bewildered by the upheaval in his life.

You should bring a few clothes and toys to the airport. If your child arrives in winter be sure to include a coat, hat, blanket (depending on the age), and so on. Even relatively warm parts of the U.S. will seem cold to a child from a tropical country. Good toy choices include stuffed animals for babies and toddlers and books with colorful pictures for toddlers and older children. Be sure to photograph your child's arrival. You will treasure these pictures for the rest of your life.

## FOREIGN TRAVEL

If you have to travel to a foreign country, you should receive detailed instructions as to when you have to be there and what you need to do while you are there. A representative of the foreign adoption program should be available to assist you in your dealings with government adoption officials, language barriers, and your stay in the country.

Generally you are responsible for your own air travel arrangements. Some agencies have guest houses or recommend inexpensive hotels. However, you can choose your own hotel and make other arrangements as you would for any trip abroad.

Some countries require only one trip to complete adoption. Ideally, you will be told how long you must stay, but sometimes estimates are erroneous. Other countries require either a stay of six to eight weeks for local adoption processing or two trips to complete the process. If a couple is adopting, sometimes only one must go. On the first trip, you can expect to meet the child, be interviewed by local social workers, and file your application. You may appear in court and might meet the birth parent(s). On the second trip, you appear in court to finalize the adoption and complete immigration arrangements for your child.

Flexibility is the key to surviving a trip abroad to bring home a child. If possible, talk to someone from the nation you will be visiting or an agency staff member familiar with the country about such things as appropriate attire for any hearings or court appearances, climate, tipping, gratuities to orphanages, and so on.

Depending on where you have to go, you might be tempted to consider this trip a vacation. This is a mistake. You are probably headed for one of the most stressful adventures of your life. Some agencies will have your time fairly tightly scheduled. Plans may even include some sightseeing and shopping. Many days will be devoted to getting to know your child, attending hearings and waiting in government offices to process paperwork.

Do not expect a warm welcome from your child. She doesn't even know you. You are uprooting her from the only home she has ever known. Depending on her age and living situation, she may be fearful, depressed, indifferent, or even hostile. This can be a very difficult time for all involved.

You may be exhausted and having trouble adjusting to the strange food, culture, and climate. Your child's caretakers may be grief stricken over her imminent departure. Even when you know you are doing the best thing for this child, such circumstances are distressing. You may have brief "second thoughts" but those probably will disappear once the trip is over. You will need all the strength and patience you can muster. At least you know it will all be over in a few days.

## COMING HOME

We suggest that you take the quickest possible route home. Stops along the way just add to your child's exhaustion and confusion. He needs to get to his new home as quickly as possible to begin adjusting to his new life. He needs to develop a sense of identity and permanence again.

Try to travel home on a weekday when flights are less crowded. Ask for aisle and window seats with the middle seat left vacant so your child can sleep much of the way. You will forever bless any airline that makes such arrangements.

Your child will travel to the U.S. with his nation's passport. When you arrive in this country, in addition to collecting your baggage and clearing Customs, you will have to go through Immigration at an American international airport. This is a fairly simple matter of presenting documents and giving your home address to which the child's "Green Card" should be sent. All permanent alien residents of the U.S. carry this card until they become citizens. Warn anyone meeting you to expect to wait at least an extra half an hour.

## POSTSCRIPT

Many women who have given birth say that they would never have become pregnant had they known what labor would be like, but that they forget most of the pain when their baby is born. The adoptive process is a little like this. When you are going through it the first time, you may marvel at how anyone ever makes it. The wait may seem endless, the complications horrendous. But once you have your child, you forget how long a year or eighteen months was. All you know is that you have your child now and forever. It's why you see so many families with more than one foreign adopted child, even though many found the second or succeeding adoptions even more difficult than the first.

CHAPTER 7

# Winning at Adoption

Now that we've given you basic information about foreign adoption, it's time to play The Foreign Adoption Game. Unlike Monopoly, it doesn't come in a box with neatly printed instructions. However, there are rules and players who win or lose. The stakes are infinitely higher than Boardwalk or Park Place.

In this chapter, we will see how the game works when a fictitious typical couple, Bill and Mary Smith, play it with their social worker, Sally Jones.

## THE FOREIGN ADOPTION GAME

**Objective:** The purpose of this game is to place a child in the home of an adoptive family. The game ends when a child is adopted.

**Players:** Prospective adoptive parents, social workers, and foreign adoption officials.

**Scoring:** This game is based on cooperation. The social worker is the referee and the scorekeeper. Foreign adoption officials can withdraw from or change the game at any time for any reason. There are no appeals from these decisions. Parents score points when their moves bring them closer to adoption. They lose points when they alienate their social worker, agency, or foreign adoption sources so badly that adoption is delayed.

**Rules:**
1. Social workers and foreign adoption officials make the rules. The prospective parents play by them.

2. Parents learn the rules by playing the game. Often they discover they have broken a rule only when they are penalized.
3. Parents score or lose points based on their ability to know when and how to push ahead and when to drop back and let events take their course.
4. Foreign adoption officials can make "wild moves" at any time. They can speed up the game, slow it down, or cancel it entirely.
5. Prospective parents and social workers can only react to such moves. They can't "checkmate" them.
6. If Wild Moves by foreign adoption officials cause parents to lose a round, they can earn points with their social worker by graciously accepting defeat. These points carry over to the next round and can lead to a relatively quick victory.

## PLAYING THE FOREIGN ADOPTION GAME

Bill and Mary Smith are a childless couple in their thirties. They are healthy and have been happily married for five years. They have a nice home and a good income. Bill is an accountant. Mary is high school English teacher. Bill is a United Methodist, Mary is a Catholic.

Mary has been unable to conceive despite a year of fertility treatments. She has talked Bill into trying to adopt after a sermon at church about the needs of children in Latin America. Bill still isn't sure about adoption.

Their social worker, Sally Jones, is also in her thirties. She's a single mother with two children whom she struggles to support on a social worker's modest salary. Her agency, Adorable Child International, provides an excellent service, but Sally and her co-workers are perennially overworked. Sally normally has a case load of about thirty families. She also conducts monthly adoption inquiry workshops on her "day off." Her phone rings forty-five or fifty times a day.

She's dedicated to her job, but at times she's so tired she can barely make it through the day. She stays with adoption work mostly because of the rewards of placing children in good homes. Her bulletin board is full of pictures of children she has placed and notes from grateful parents.

During the next year, Sally will become the most important outsider in the Smiths' lives. At times, their relationship will be tense. The Smiths will resent the power that Sally has over them while understanding that they are dependent on her.

## FIRST MEETING

Bill and Mary are nervous about their first meeting with Sally. They take time off work. They worry about what to wear. What kind of impression should they make? Bill opts for a sports coat and tie, Mary for a dress and blazer. To Sally, they look responsible and pleasant. Score one for the Smiths.

The meeting itself is awkward. Sally tries to put the Smiths at ease, but she's preoccupied by a crisis involving an adoptive family in Guatemala. Although Sally normally has her calls held during such meetings, she instructs her secretary to put through any calls from the family or the agency in Guatemala City. During the Smiths' half-hour appointment, there are three.

Sally apologizes to the Smiths, but her mind is elsewhere. Bill and Mary sense that they are just one more couple to Sally and they aren't sure what to think. Bill suggests waiting a few more months to see if Mary gets pregnant, but Mary is determined to proceed. They make appointments for home study interviews.

## THE HOME STUDY

Like most prospective adoptive parents, the Smiths dread the home study. They don't know what to expect or how they will be judged. They are afraid to ask the agency and no one volunteers the criteria for a high score. These include:

- Having no obvious impediments such as poor health, a police record, or several previous marriages.
- Being warm and loving.
- Being flexible.
- Having a home that is safe and decent.
- Understanding that, like it or not, they must cooperate with the adoption process.

- Realizing that above all, the caseworker is looking for families that seem "safe." This means projecting an aura of stability and responsibility. The more mainstream the parents seem, the better their chances are.

Let's see how the Smiths did.

## Obvious Impediments

When Sally meets a new couple or single parent, she instinctively gives them a "once over" which includes a practiced ability to detect prospective parents who are obviously unsuitable for adoption. She tries not to let her first judgment bias her study, but it has some impact. She would not assume that her best friend would be qualified to adopt. She insists that all prospective parents go through the full study.

She asks Mary and Bill to have their doctor submit basic information on their health and to submit to a police check, which requires them to go to a police station for fingerprinting.

These requests help initiate Mary and Bill to the loss of privacy entailed in a home study. They understand the reason for the health request even as they feel somewhat invaded. The police check offends Bill.

"I can't believe we have to do this," grumbles Bill after leaving Sally's office. "Can't she see we're respectable? After all, I was president of our neighborhood association last year and you were Washington High's outstanding teacher. What more do they want?"

Mary, too, is appalled. Being fingerprinted by a uniformed officer in such a setting makes her feel vaguely criminal even though she has nothing to fear. She doubts that two parking tickets in ten years will keep her from adopting.

Mary is determined to do whatever it takes to adopt. "Once we have a child, we'll either forget about this or laugh about it," she tells Bill over coffee. "Remember the guy in New York who abused and murdered his daughter? He seemed to be as respectable as we are. I can see why they have to be careful. Besides, we have no choice if we want to adopt."

**Scoring:** As she expected, Sally finds no obvious impediments. She gives the Smiths top marks.

## Warmth

Mary and Bill faced their individual interviews with Sally with some trepidation. Both came away relieved. Sally had been pleasant, even encouraging. Mostly she wanted to know why they wanted to adopt. In such sessions, Sally deliberately affected a comfortable manner to encourage confidences, but she continued to listen for possible problems.

Mary exuded warmth in her interview, as she does in life.

"I seem to attract the stray kids at school," Mary said. "You know, the girls who don't get dates to the prom and the guys who can't make the varsity. I'm not supposed to know that my nickname is 'Mother Mary.'

"I've always loved helping these kids, but now I want a permanent relationship with a child. I adore my mom. I want to do the same things with a kid that she did with us. I want to hang stockings at Christmas and take long walks in the park. I get jealous when my friends complain about the noise and mess their kids make. I'd give *anything* for some noise and mess."

Sally smiled encouragingly. It was a story (with variations) she'd heard many times.

Bill was less effusive, but tried to conceal his doubts about adoption.

"I guess I want to adopt because Mary wants to so badly. It kills me to see Mary watching every baby we see and thinking 'if only.' I'll do whatever it takes to make her happy.

"I'm not as good at talking as Mary. I'm trying to picture myself as a father. I think I'll like it. At least I hope so."

**Scoring:** Sally gives the Smiths, especially Mary, high marks for warmth. Mary's longing for a child is desperately obvious. Sally is a bit concerned, but not terribly bothered by Bill's reserve. Such hesitancy on the part of one parent is not unusual this early in the process. However, she makes a mental note to see if Bill warms up and grows more enthusiastic as time goes on and questions are answered.

**Commentary:** One of the hardest parts of Sally's job is playing judge and counselor simultaneously. She has to encourage parents to reveal enough of themselves so that she can begin judging whether they would be good parents. Yet they know they are being judged. This tends to make them somewhat reserved and fearful.

Sally relies on her experience to detect insincerity or lack of the caring that is essential to be a good parent. Don't worry if you are naturally reserved (as long as it isn't so extreme you can't communicate with other people). Some of the best parents have a quiet warmth and sincerity. Try to be yourself.

## Flexibility

When Mary and Bill walked into Adorable Child International, Mary knew precisely what kind of child she wanted to adopt: a healthy baby girl from Central America. Sally tried to interest the Smiths in other options, including boys, slightly older children, and children from other regions.

"You might even want to think about a child with a slight handicap since you have excellent insurance," Sally said. "If you're open to more types of children, you may get a child sooner."

But Mary was adamant. She had a strong sense that she was supposed to adopt a Central American baby girl. Since Adorable Child International had a program in only one Central American country, Sally put the Smiths on that list with their specifications underlined.

**Scoring:** Mary and Bill lose points with their determination to accept only a very specific type of child. Sally is limited in her ability to search for a child for them. She also wonders if they might be too rigid to make good foreign adoptive parents.

**Commentary:** Parents have a right to specify what type of child they wish to adopt. However, the more open they are to various options, the faster they are likely to get a child. It's okay to hold out for a child of a particular age, sex, or nationality as long as you realize the consequences. It's also good to explain to your social worker *why* you feel so strongly about your choice.

More parents request girls than boys. Apparently more people believe that a foreign adopted girl will be better accepted than a boy. People who will accept a boy are likely to get a boy and get him sooner than those who insist on a girl.

Some people say they can't accept a child from "X" country because the child will not be accepted by the community. This causes the social worker to wonder if it is the parents or the community that cannot accept a certain type of child.

People willing to adopt older children will find a plentiful supply. Social workers understand a desire for a baby or young child and will not try to pressure parents into accepting an older child.

Social workers will nearly always explore the idea of a special needs adoption but usually won't try to pressure parents who aren't interested. You shouldn't adopt a child with special needs unless you feel capable of coping with the demands.

A request for a healthy child is normal and acceptable. It's also okay to insist on a particular country, especially if you have a good reason such as relatives or friends from that country or previous residence there. Most social workers will be very receptive to such reasons because they help promote a successful adoption experience.

Don't be pressured into changing your specifications in order to get a child sooner. Just be aware of alternatives and the consequences of your request.

## Decent Home

Before Sally's visit, Mary cleaned her suburban ranch-style house from top to bottom. She even vacuumed behind the family-room couch and begged Bill to wash the picture window inside and out.

"What if it rains?" he asked. "Do you really think clean windows will help us get a kid?"

"Wash," ordered Mary.

When Sally arrived, the house was spotless. The fenced-in back yard was newly mowed and the dog was asleep in a corner of the kitchen.

"I see we both like antiques," said Sally brightly as she mentally checked off her list:

- Could the house be child-proofed?
- Was there a safe place to play?
- Did the Smiths keep poisons where a child could get to them?
- Was the house in good repair?
- Was there a bedroom for the child?

Sally couldn't help kidding the Smiths a bit. "Are you always this neat?"

**Scoring:** Sally tries to fight her envy of the Smith home. It is much nicer than hers. She's relieved that the Smiths haven't decorated a nursery yet, like some prospective parents.

**Commentary:** It isn't necessary to have a model suburban home to adopt a child. Children don't have to have their own bedrooms. City apartments with parks in the area are acceptable. Most adoptive parents aren't perfect housekeepers. Social workers may even worry if things seem so perfect that a child would disrupt the perfection.

Social workers are looking for homes that are decent and comfortable. Before the social worker arrives, clean and tidy up. Don't start any renovation projects (some people do). Be sure all hazardous and poisonous substances are locked up and obvious safety problems such as loose electrical cords are eliminated.

If you have a pet, try to keep it from disrupting the visit. A dog that is howling because it is confined to the garage might be better allowed to come in. If the pet can't behave either indoors or outside, take it to the kennel for the afternoon.

You can play background music but keep it quiet. Avoid special types of music unless you know your taste matches that of your social worker. Easy Listening anything will do just fine. You don't want to risk raising unnecessary questions or inadvertently offending. Feel free to offer the social worker non-alcoholic refreshments but don't insist she accept.

## Financial Ability to Raise a Child

"Do they really need to know how much money we earn and what our total assets are?" asked Bill. "I hate giving out that kind of confidential information. Is it really any of their business? We don't exactly look destitute."

"They just need to know we can afford this child," said Mary. "Remember, they've probably run into people who looked like they were doing great but were in debt up to their eyeballs. I hate this part of it too. I have to get a letter from my principal, and that means I have to tell her we're adopting.

"What if she spreads it around school? I don't want half the faculty asking me every other day if we've heard anything."

Although they found it distasteful, both got Sally the letters she needed.

**Scoring:** Sally never was worried that the Smiths couldn't afford a child, but the letters document the case. She had previously approved many couples with incomes less than half of theirs.

**Commentary:** Although most adoptive parents hate disclosing confidential financial information, they are required to do so. Agencies and foreign governments insist on evidence that parents can afford to raise their child. Parents will be asked about their incomes and assets, but not their expenses or debts.

Some agencies want at least one parent to stay home for a time, but working adoptive mothers are a fact of life, just like working birth mothers. If you must promise to stay home, agree to do so without specifying how long. Increasing numbers of employers grant paid or unpaid parental leave to adopt a child. Ask your employer.

## Cooperation

"How many more workshops do we have to go to?" grumbled Bill when Mary told him to reserve Saturday morning for a group session on "Coping with a Foreign Culture."

"This is the last one we have to go to for the home study," Mary assured him. "I'm tired of them too, and I have a ton of term papers to grade. But we have to suffer through."

Mary doesn't mind attending the workshop, but she figures she had better show some empathy for Bill. He has grumbled, but so far he's done everything the social worker has asked.

Mary and Bill arrive late for the workshop and leave the moment they decently can. Mary hopes that Sally hasn't noticed, but she has.

Sally, in fact, has picked up enough signals of uncertainty and even resentment on Bill's part that she's rethinking her original assessment of the couple. She calls Bill that night and says she wants to meet with him.

At the meeting, she's kind but firm.

"I have noticed that you don't seem very enthusiastic about what we're doing," she says. "We're at a point now when I need to know where you stand. Is this something you want to do or isn't it? Foreign adoption isn't for everyone, and it may not be for you. I know how Mary feels but before you and I spend more time, I need to know how *you* feel. You're going to be a parent as much as she is."

For a moment, Bill is silent. Sally has hit him hard. He's a little frightened of becoming a father. He hates the adoption process, but he does want a child. He wants one more than he has ever admitted, even to himself, until now. Words don't come easily to Bill. Sally studies his reactions carefully.

"I guess, no, I know I want this kid," he said slowly. "I've never had to go to things like these meetings. I feel funny talking to complete strangers about my feelings. But I do want a child. I've sort of gotten used to thinking what our house will be like when we get a kid. I'll never like your meetings or the paperwork, but you've made me realize how bad I would feel if we didn't get a child."

"That's good enough for me," said Sally.

**Scoring:** Bill and Mary came close to losing it all when Sally grew seriously concerned about Bill's commitment to adopting. He was saved by her willingness to talk things over. Some social workers might have dropped or downgraded the couple without making that extra effort.

**Commentary:** Longsuffering is a virtue that adoptive parents must acquire. It is best to do what needs to be done and hide any resentment. If you can't abide your agency, try to find another you will like better. That may be impossible. If you do start agency shopping, don't tell your original agency until your new agency has agreed to work with you. You could find yourself back on square one.

Sally felt it was critical to confront Bill because she had to find out if his behavior was a subtle way of saying he didn't want to adopt, and he didn't want to tell a social worker he didn't want to adopt. Some prospective parents prefer to place the burden of refusal on the social worker and the social agency to avoid problems with their spouses. Sally had to find out if Bill was trying to do this. He persuaded her he was not.

## Stability and Respectability

Sally has asked Mary and Bill to submit three letters of recommendation from friends, and one each from a clergyperson and a doctor. The letters help Sally complete the portrait of the prospective parents that she has developed from her interviews. She needs them to determine what type of reputation Mary and Bill enjoy. Friends can supply insights that may help her understand things she has observed or comments in interviews.

Mary and Bill think carefully about their choices. They select their best man, who is a successful local stockbroker, a beloved next-door neighbor, and Mary's best friend at school.

Since Mary and Bill are of different faiths, they ask a nun whom they both know from volunteer tutoring to write their clergy letter. Their family doctor certifies their good health and mentions Mary's infertility treatments.

**Scoring:** Mary and Bill receive glowing letters from everyone. Sally is well satisfied.

**Commentary:** Veteran social workers often are amazed at what they learn in the letters, especially since the parents select the authors. Sometimes they are informed of problems that had eluded them.

Your letters should come from people who know you well enough to give detailed information about your lives. Vague letters of praise from important people are useless.

Some countries and agencies require proof of infertility. A doctor's letter is usually sufficient.

## COMPOSITE SCORE: THE HOME STUDY

Sally gives Mary and Bill high marks. She informs them that they are on the waiting list for a child from Central America.

At this point, Sally and the Smiths have a cautiously friendly relationship. The Smiths are convinced that the worst part of the Adoption Game is over. They soon find out that it has barely begun.

### Waiting

In a hurried phone conversation, Sally tells Mary to expect at least a six-month wait for a referral. She warns that it could be longer since they insist on a healthy infant girl from just one part of the world.

Unfortunately, all Mary hears is "six months." Sally forgets to mention how long the wait is likely to be after a baby is assigned. Mary hangs up and tells Bill "in six months, we'll have a baby."

For five months, Sally hears nothing from the Smiths. Finally Mary calls to see if anything is happening. Sally says no.

A month later, Bill calls Sally. He is excited.

"The six months are up. Do you have our baby?"

"We still don't know anything."

"You said it would be six months. We were counting on that."

"Six months is only approximate. That was our best guess. I promise to let you know the minute we hear anything," Sally responds.

"Are you sure you don't know anything?" asks Bill. "One of the other couples in our orientation class already has a child. We saw them at a basketball game."

"The Hansons said they would take the first child of either sex under ten who became available from any country," said Sally, losing patience. "Josh is a seven-year-old Korean boy with a hearing problem. It takes longer when you want a specific type of child. Have your changed your minds about that?"

"No," said Bill. "But we want her so badly. I hope you can hurry things."

"I'm doing the best I can," sighs Sally.

Sally hopes this will end the matter, but it doesn't. Mary is positive that Sally told her they would have a baby in six months, and they don't. Something must be the matter. Mary thinks maybe it's because she's handled most of the dealings with the agency and they don't feel they have to pay attention to a woman. She urges Bill to call Sally's boss.

Bill does so, offering a large donation to move things faster. Sally's boss calls her in to discuss the Smiths.

"Are you sure they would be good parents? I can understand impatience, but bribery is something else. Maybe you should reconsider their application."

Sally is furious. She calls Bill.

She says she feels that he has broken faith with her by going to her boss. He's made her look bad and she doesn't like it, not one bit. She tells Bill how close he has come to being disqualified.

Bill is almost equally angry. He can't see why what he has done is so awful. He's pretty sure that agencies give preference to big givers. He's in business and wasn't born yesterday. But he's scared. He realizes that he has broken an important rule that no one told him was there.

Bill finally understands that he and Mary are at the mercy of the agency and that adoption does not work like a business.

"If we didn't want that kid so badly and if we had any other choice, I'd never put up with this," he tells Mary. But they both realize the only alternative is to start the game over—a devastating prospect.

For several weeks, Sally and the Smiths avoid each other. They know there is no point in calling her, and she wants them to know she is still unhappy. She could have made a few calls on their behalf to see if things were moving, but she decides to let nature take its course.

**Scoring:** This was a terrible round for the Smiths. They learned some of the rules and the consequences of breaking them. At least they are still in the game.

**Commentary:** Often it is very hard for adoptive parents to accept being powerless. They try to influence events with disastrous results. To win, they must learn how to apply pressure without offending those who control the action. This could involve making polite calls every other week to see how things are coming, sending notes expressing eagerness for a child or sending photos. *Polite persistence pays off.*

If the wife has handled most arrangements, she should continue to do so. A social worker might interpret a sudden call from the husband as a power play.

## A Baby Is Assigned

Eight months after completing the Smiths' home study, Sally calls Mary's school and leaves an urgent message for her to call immediately.

"I think I have a baby girl for you!" she said ten minutes later when Mary returns the call. "Can you or Bill come to discuss this? I've put a hold on her, but you have to accept her."

"Shall I come now?" said Mary. "I can be there in half an hour."

"Slow down," said Sally. "After school would be fine. How about 4:00 P.M.? Would Bill like to join us?"

"We'll be there."

Trembling, Mary calls Bill immediately.

"Sally just called," she says. "We've got a girl! We can meet Sally at four at her office to discuss it."

The rest of the day passes in a blur. Mary wants to laugh and cry and hug everyone.

"Are you okay, Mrs. Smith?" asks one of her junior boys after she started giggling in the middle of class. "Did I say something funny?"

At 4:00 P.M., Mary and Bill walk into Sally's office. It looks different from the last time they were there. The receptionist greets them warmly. Sally is beaming.

"What do you think?" she asks proudly as she hands them a tiny picture of a baby with huge dark eyes and a wisp of dark hair.

Mary had been prepared to say any baby was beautiful but *this* little girl is obviously someone special. Mary beams at Bill, Bill beams at Mary and they both try to figure out what to say.

"I take it you like her," Sally says. "I was pretty sure you would. I'll give you the information I've got. It's never as much as you'd like, but it's all good in this case. We know, at least, that she's healthy. She's six months old and has been in the orphanage since birth. That's good. They take good care of the kids there even though there are no extras."

After Mary and Bill sign a form accepting their daughter, Sally returns to the business of adoption.

"Here are the documents you will need to prepare for the courts," she says. "I've checked the ones that I take care of. You get the rest back to me as soon as possible. Then we'll talk about what comes next."

"How soon will it be before we get Christina?" asked Bill. "That's what we're going to call her."

"I'd hate to guess," says Sally. "Nine months from the time you get your papers in until you go to get her is about average. That means it could be anywhere from six months to a year. A lot depends on when you get the papers in and if the court takes any kind of a holiday recess. I'm reluctant to predict these things."

"You mean it could be that long to get her?" said Bill. His disappointment is obvious. Now that he has actually seen his daughter, Sally can see that his eagerness matches that of his wife.

"Isn't there anything we can do to speed this up—I mean without getting in trouble?" asks Bill. "I could call our congressman. He's on the Foreign Affairs Committee. Maybe he could speed things up. That is, if it's okay with you."

"Sorry," said Sally. "We have to respect their procedures. If you try that, you could lose Christina and we'd never get another child out of that country. It's hard to be patient, but you don't have much choice."

"Okay," says Bill. "You're the expert. We won't do anything without checking with you."

After hugs and congratulations, the Smiths leave Sally's office both thrilled and disappointed. They have their daughter, but the hardest part of their wait is beginning. This time they follow Sally's instructions to the letter. Mary returns the documents four days later along with a thank-you note and a homemade coffee cake.

Four months later, she calls to ask if Sally has heard anything. Sally says no, but suggests she call in another month. Mary does so. This time, Sally promises to call the orphanage to see if anything is happening. Mary expresses appreciation.

Sally makes several calls and finds that a key document has been mislaid. Her call puts things back on schedule. Sally calls Mary to report.

"It looks like we should have good news in a couple of weeks," says Sally. "I'll keep you posted."

Mary buys an answering machine to make sure they don't miss a call from Sally. She and Bill stop going out to dinner—just in case. They leave strict instructions at work to summon them the instant Sally calls. Every time the phone rings, Mary wonders if it might be Sally.

Three and a half weeks later, the phone was ringing as Mary came home from school.

"How soon can you leave for Central America?" asks Sally.

**Scoring:** Mary and Bill learned a lot from their blunder. They played this round perfectly. Mary's homemade coffee cake paid big dividends as did her occasional calls.

**Commentary:** Polite persistence pays. Never give up hope—and never give up!

74

## Travel

During the eight months they waited to get Christina, Bill and Mary filed documents with the U.S. Immigration and Naturalization Service to admit their daughter to the United States. Before leaving, they notified INS to cable this permission to the U.S. Embassy. They also read up on their destination and selected a hotel near Christina's orphanage. Mary brushed up on her Spanish, and both renewed their passports. All they needed after Sally's call were their tickets.

Sally had helped prepare them for the trip by giving them the name of another family that had adopted from their country. The Sunday afternoon the Smiths spent with Don and Marge Anderson and their son Robert was extremely helpful. The Andersons told them what kinds of gifts to take for which people, what clothing to take, and what kinds of activities to expect. It had also helped to see Robert—a chubby, friendly three-year-old.

Mary and Bill did not know how long they would have to stay. Sally said she hoped it would be only about two weeks, but it could be more or less. Sally warned them not to try to speed up the host country's procedures.

Their flight from Miami was routine. They caught a cab to their hotel and wondered what would happen next. Mary was unpacking when the phone rang.

"We get to see her in an hour?"

"Sí," a cheerful voice replied.

"Bill, we get to see her in an hour. Let's go!"

Both forgot their exhaustion, hastily changed clothes and hailed a cab. They hardly noticed the street vendors, the great cathedral, and the central market. All they could think about was Christina!

The orphanage was a pleasant but modest building on a side street. Several older children played tag in the front yard. A pleasant woman, the director, greeted them. Christina, age fourteen months, was waiting in the nursery. Orphanage workers had dressed her up to meet her new parents. She sat calmly in a staff member's lap eating a banana as the worker talked soothingly to her in Spanish. Then the worker held her out to Mary.

"Mama," the worker repeated over and over. "Mama."

"Christina," murmured Mary softly, unaware that she was weeping. "Christina."

At first Christina seemed bewildered and resisted being handed over. The worker continued to encourage her to go to Mary, who dug into her purse for a piece of candy. Christina finally allowed Mary and then Bill to hold her but soon grew restless. She wanted to play!

Mary set her on the floor and began to play patty cake while Bill got out the camera. Then Christina smiled! It was a beautiful smile that lighted up her entire face. Her big dark eyes sparkled.

"Gato," she squealed as the orphanage cat wandered in. "Gato!"

While Mary played with Christina and the cat, and Bill took Polaroid pictures of the children and staff (a marvelous icebreaker in any country), Mary tried to learn as much as she could about Christina.

It was obvious that she was healthy and lively. Staff members assured the new parents that she was happy, got along with other children, and had a healthy appetite—especially for sweets.

Although Mary and Bill wanted to take their daughter with them that minute, they knew they couldn't. Christina would stay at the orphanage until after the court hearing.

But as Mary and Bill left the orphanage that day, with instructions to return the next morning for a trip to the central market to buy new clothes for Christina, they had fallen madly in love with their daughter. She had already become theirs.

"I never imagined it would be like this," said Mary in the cab back to the hotel. "She's so much more beautiful than her pictures. Did you ever see a smile like that?" Bill, too, was overwhelmed, his feelings too deep for words. But there was a new gentleness as he stroked Mary's hair.

"Where do you think we should send her to college?" he asked. "I can see how bright she is. Harvard is expensive. Maybe we should start saving." Over a quiet celebration dinner, Mary and Bill studied their itinerary for the days ahead.

They found that the greatest delay seemed to be with an appointment at the American Embassy made by a local social worker for a week after their court hearing.

"I think we should try to get this moved up a week," said Bill. "After all, we're dealing with the American Embassy." Mary agreed.

They called the embassy and explained the situation to an immigration worker.

"No problem," said a midwestern voice. "When would you folks like to come? We're open from 9:00 A.M. to 4:00 P.M. weekdays." Mary asked for a 9:30 A.M. appointment the day after their court hearing.

"It takes us a day after your appointment to process your papers," the official said. "You can leave anytime after that. We have your cable from INS on file."

Mary and Bill spent the rest of the trip getting acquainted with Christina and following the local agency's instructions to the letter.

Mary and Bill found their parental instincts taking over. Christina seemed to understand their hugs, kisses, games, and even their chatter. Mary, the teacher, would use a familiar Spanish word, then its English counterpart and point at the object. Since Christina was mostly babbling, the mixture of languages caused no problems.

"Gato," Mary said when she petted the cat. "That means cat, Christina. When you get home, you can have your own cat. We already have a perro. That's a dog."

Mary and Bill used Christina's new name frequently to help her get accustomed to it. Staff members stopped calling her Elena, the name her birth mother had given her.

The social workers from the orphanage were helpful. The delays at the court were what they had been warned to expect. But all in all, things went fairly smoothly.

**Scoring:** Mary and Bill did well. They scored many points by realizing when they had to follow instructions and when it was okay to try to make other arrangements.

**Commentary:** Americans who travel to other countries to adopt children must be very sensitive to the feelings of their hosts. However, when they are dealing with American Embassy rules, they are free to politely act like Americans dealing with any government office in the U.S. They should realize that foreign social workers may be intimidated by American Embassy personnel, but this does not mean they must be.

## HOMECOMING

About eighteen months after their first visit with Sally, Mary and Bill stepped off a plane, carrying Christina. Sally saw them in their home a few days later. She sensed their joy the minute she walked in the door.

The Smiths' formerly immaculate house was comfortably cluttered with Christina's new toys. A high chair had been placed at the kitchen table. A large color photo of Christina dominated the piano.

The phone rang frequently with congratulatory calls. A "Welcome Home Christina" bouquet graced the dining-room table. The newest member of the family sat on her mother's lap munching a cookie while her father played peek-a-boo with her. Both could hardly take their eyes off their daughter—except when one of them reached for the camera.

"We're buying stock in film," Mary joked. "We've filled two albums already. Of course that includes our pictures of the trip and Christina's homecoming. What do you think of the teddy bear from my folks? It's bigger than she is. My dad brought it to the airport."

Sally asked a few questions for her report, but mostly she just visited with the Smiths. She admired Christina and the nursery stacked high with gifts. It was a story she had seen many times before, yet each tale was new and infinitely special.

"I've got the best job in the world," she thought as she drove away.

## SUMMARY

The Adoption Game is hard on everyone while it is in progress. It is infinitely satisfying after it is over. In general, parents should:

- Assume that their social worker has their best interests at heart unless they have evidence to the contrary. If this is the case, they should change workers or agencies.
- Assume that most things will take longer than anticipated. They should allow at least an extra week after the stated deadline, then check on what's happening.

- Understand that foreign governments are under no pressure to move American adoption cases quickly. They just have to accept this.
- Have hope. If they're qualified to adopt and work with a good agency, they'll eventually win, as thousands of others have.

## POSTSCRIPT

Once a child is placed in your home, the Adoption Game is nearly over. You may be required to attend a postplacement session or two with your agency, and your social worker will have to report to the court before you can finalize the adoption. However, if all goes well, those will be either helpful opportunities or mere formalities.

In most cases, the finalization of an adoption ends formal contact with the agency. However, parents may want to visit the agency or send pictures. Sending pictures via the agency back to the foreign country helps cement good feelings between American and foreign adoption workers. This can be a big help next time you decide to play the Foreign Adoption Game!

CHAPTER 8

# We Have a Child!

Your dream has come true! Your long-awaited child has come home. You should be ecstatically happy and maybe you are. But maybe you aren't. No matter how badly you wanted your child, you may find the adjustment to parenthood more difficult than you had imagined it would be. You may even think there is something wrong with you. Maybe you even panic and wonder if you did the right thing in adopting.

Chances are excellent you didn't make a mistake. It takes time to adjust to parenting almost any child, especially one who is adapting to a major upheaval in her life.

In this chapter we will discuss:

- Preparing for your child's homecoming
- Things no one ever thought to tell you
- Bonding with your child
- Discipline
- Completing your adoption
- Naturalization
- Disruptions

## PREPARING FOR THE HOMECOMING

When you accept your child's referral, you will be given basic information such as age, sex, and approximate health status. Based on that, you can start planning for your child's arrival. You may delay some specific arrangements (such as child care) until you know the arrival date. We suggest that you prepare a checklist containing these items.

## Room

You will have to prepare a bedroom for your child unless he or she will be sharing a room with a brother or sister. It is wise to start off with just the basics in furniture, toys, and decorations, especially if you are adopting an older child with well-developed tastes. You will have a better feel for how your child's room should look after he or she arrives. Friends with children of about the same age can tell you what's "in" and offer suggestions on equipment.

## Clothes

Purchase only one or two outfits for your child to wear immediately after arrival. Chances are your child will be a different size than you anticipated. If you are adopting a baby, you will need at least a few diapers to get started. Even diapers come in different sizes, though, so you should wait until your child arrives before buying too many.

## Insurance

Check with your employer or insurance agent before your child arrives about when you can add him to your family policy. Many companies require proof that you have custody of the child before providing coverage. If (heaven forbid) your child requires medical attention before you've filed these papers, these costs may not be covered. (See chapter 5 on adoption finances.)

## Parental Leave

Check with your employer (if you work outside the home) about what leave you may be entitled to. Some enlightened employers allow parental leave for adoptions. However, most companies do not—even if they offer paid maternity leave to pregnant employees. The difference? Giving birth is considered a temporary physical disability and treated like any other disability. Since adoption involves no physical disability, it isn't covered. You may, however, be able to get unpaid leave or vacation.

## Child Care

If you plan to return to work fairly soon after your child arrives, it is good to begin searching for child care as soon as you know approximately when you will need it. Finding a caregiver can be difficult. It can consume hours which you should be spending with your child after her arrival. Your best referrals often come by word of mouth. Start asking friends for recommendations. Look for a setting where your child will receive lots of warmth and one-to-one attention. Spend some time checking it out.

## Toys

Check with friends who have children about the age of your child for suggestions about appropriate toys, but don't buy anything elaborate until your child arrives. Even a toddler will delight in a toy shopping expedition. If you are adopting a toddler or an older child, look for items that will help him or her learn English, such as simple colorful books, classic cartoon videotapes, and educational (but entertaining) audiotapes or CDs. Your public library will have many such items available.

## THINGS NO ONE EVER THOUGHT TO TELL YOU

Your first days as a parent will very likely be filled with surprises, depending on the age of your child and the country from which he came. Here are examples of some of the surprises that adoptive families often encounter.

## Food

- Asian babies often are allergic to cow's milk. Soy milk is a good, readily available substitute.
- Bananas are an outstanding "transition" food for children of any age. Other good choices include fruits and fruit juice, ice cream, rice, cereal, nuts, yogurt, and toast.
- Your child will either arrive addicted to soda or soon acquire the taste.
- Junk food will make a much bigger hit than most healthy foods.

82

## Health

Your child will need a medical checkup soon after arrival. Ask the doctor to check for parasites and to be alert for symptoms of other illnesses uncommon among middle-class American children. Have the doctor do a Hepatitis B screen and surfaced-core antigene. A study of foreign adopted children found that a significant percentage have illnesses that can be detected only by such tests.

Ask your agency to provide you or your doctor with information about what conditions to look for. These include common illnesses in the native land. Ask your doctor to try to locate a physician or medical student from that country for more information about health conditions. If your child has a disability you didn't expect, don't panic. Seek further help and counseling, especially if your doctor mentions frightening possibilities such as mental retardation. Children can be misdiagnosed, especially under these circumstances.

## Schedule

Your child's timetable will be completely out of sync. It will take five to six dreadful days to get him sleeping at night instead of during the day.

The best way to get the days and nights straightened out is to be very firm. No matter how hard your child cries, insist that he stay in bed at night. Wake him up in the morning and keep him from taking long afternoon naps. You may feel like a child abuser, but this is something you *have* to do. Crying never killed a child.

## Possessions

If you adopt an older child who has been in an orphanage, expect her to be extremely possessive of her things. She has been so deprived that she will cling to everything.

Don't be surprised if you find your child hiding food or refusing to surrender it after he has finished eating. Eileen will never forget the time Raj insisted on keeping his banana during his bath. Such behavior is likely to end when the child learns that there is plenty of food.

## Clothing

Don't be shocked if your child seems unfamiliar with shoes. Children from poor tropical countries seldom wear them. Toddlers who've never worn shoes may be slightly delayed in learning to walk, especially if you have hardwood floors.

In some countries, small boys don't wear pants. Diapers may be a surprise.

Expect your child from a warm climate to bundle up more than an American child. What seems pleasantly crisp to you may seem like the Arctic to him.

## Sleeping and Bathroom Arrangements

Children from orphanages have never experienced privacy. They may be afraid to sleep alone in a room. They may even feel like they are being banished. You will have to insist on the adjustment but be gentle about it.

Children from many countries have never slept in an American bed or crib before. They're used to mats on the floor. And, to your toddler, the bars on a crib might seem like a cage.

You may try letting your child go to sleep on sofa cushions on the floor. Then move him to bed and let him wake up there. He will soon get used to the change.

Expect to teach any child old enough to be toilet trained how to use an American toilet. There is no guarantee that your child has ever before used a sink, tub, or shower. A cup and a bucket are far more common in many parts of the world.

## New Name

It will take an older child or even a toddler a little time to adapt to a new name. Some children are depressed by this radical change in identity. But this will pass. Call the child by his old name *and* new name. Gradually discontinue use of the birth name.

Most Americans give their foreign adopted children American first names to aid in their adjustment. Many keep a native middle name (possibly the child's birth name). This is what Joan and Ray did.

Eileen and Ron chose foreign first names to honor their children's birth heritages. They picked names that were easy to pronounce and spell and sounded definitively masculine or feminine to Americans. They gave both children American middle names.

## New Language

Most children learn English readily, but the transition can be painful and frustrating for a few weeks or months. A conversation in the old language with a native speaker may help, or it might upset the child and offer false hope that the transition need not be made.

Help your child learn English by speaking more slowly and clearly than usual. Talk constantly to your child, naming objects and actions. ("Mommy is feeding Jessica. Jessica likes to eat bananas.") Use lots of gestures. Get other children to talk to your child. Even television can teach language.

## Brothers and Sisters

Do not expect instant rapport between new brothers and sisters even if you've prepared them for the new arrival by involving them in the home study, decorating the room, and other activities.

Expect jealousy, after the newness wears off, along with sibling rivalry and competition for your attention. Do not be surprised by remarks such as "Why did you adopt HER?"

Allow time for adjustment. Spend time alone with your other children to reassure them that your love for them hasn't changed.

When you're tempted to kill *all* your kids, remember how well you got along with your own brothers and sisters.

## BONDING WITH YOUR CHILD

One of the fears that many potential adoptive parents face is their ability to bond with their child. It is hard to voice this concern for fear of hurting your chances of getting a child, but it is nevertheless very real.

What happens if I don't like this child or if he doesn't like me?

Can I bond with an older child?

What can I do to promote bonding?

There are no simple answers to these terribly important questions. The meaning of adoption quite literally "comes home" on the journey overseas or to an airport to get the child who will be part of your life forever.

This is no longer an abstraction or a tiny face on a piece of paper. This child lives and breathes and has a personality already forming. On the trip home, you will be in many respects a different person. Although you've had months to get ready for the event, nothing has really prepared you for it.

Bonding is as individual as the people involved. With some parents and children it is instinctive and instantaneous. If you are lucky, you will feel an incredible surge of love the moment you lay eyes on your child. You will feel that this is your child forever. You will sense very soon that your child feels the same. No matter what difficulties you put each other through over the years, you are parent and child. Period.

As wonderful as this scenario sounds, it is probably the exception, especially when older children are involved. Adoptive children of any age take a bit of time to bond. In many cases they will need time and freedom to:

- Mourn the loss of the only lives they have known
- Mourn the loss of people they have loved
- Begin to know and trust you
- Begin to be happy about their new lives

If you can understand your child's need to mourn and help her through that mourning period, you will be well on your way to bonding. Your child needs you now, desperately. But it takes time for love and trust to grow. You must be strong and patient.

Some children have been emotionally harmed by having formed no early attachment to anyone. Such children may seem almost indifferent to what is happening to them. Others may go through a honeymoon phase, then start testing your commitment by acting out and manipulating their environment in any way they can. They can bring adoptive parents to the point of exhaustion and upset an entire household for months.

Parents may begin to question their parenting ability and to stifle thoughts like "I don't like this child very much" or "How long can I take this?" They may even wonder, "Why did we adopt?"

Very often such problems arise with a second adoption. The first adopted child was practically perfect, so parents thought everything would be the same with the second. They may find it takes longer to warm up to the second child, especially if he or she is older and Number One was a baby. Parents may even resent the time the second child takes from the adored first child, especially when the first child starts complaining. They may not have been prepared to cope with sibling rivalry and constant fighting (even though these are perfectly normal).

If you are having adjustment problems, ask your social worker for advice. She may recommend further help. Don't try to deny or cover up your difficulties.

Children under the age of three bond more readily than children over three because their memories are so short. Can you remember anything about what happened when you were two? Chances are you can't. It will be the same with your child. Eileen had a vivid illustration of this when Shanti was about three. As she looked at pictures taken on the trip to Thailand to adopt her, she noticed her foster mother—a woman she had adored.

"Who's that?" she asked.

"Your foster mother," Eileen replied. "You lived with her in Thailand before Daddy and I came to get you."

"Oh."

Children like Shanti who have had strong attachments may vigorously protest their loss, but they are eager to form new bonds. They respond readily to warmth and affection. There will come a time, usually after only a few months, when suddenly you realize how intense your ties to this child have become and vice versa.

Don't be dismayed if your child is initially hostile, as Shanti was. Children bond during times of intense emotion—including anger. Promote bonding through a lot of direct eye contact, even if your child is throwing a temper tantrum. The anger can be a means of testing your commitment. You need to show your child that you will be there no matter what she does.

Expect more time for bonding with older children. An older child might test your commitment or revert to a much younger stage. You may even find an older child trying to bond by attempting to nurse. Be patient. Show your child you love her no matter what, don't expect instant love in return, and know that love grows from shared experiences. Sometimes it can take two or more years for an older child to bond.

## DISCIPLINE

Initially at least, it is hard to discipline your adopted child. You have waited so long and wanted this child so badly. You understand that everything is new for the child and he has a big adjustment to make. But sooner or later, you will have to cope with the idea of discipline.

We suggest that you look at discipline in a positive light. There is an enormous difference between punishing a child and offering kind but firm direction. Your child needs such direction to adjust to her new life. You must establish yourself as your child's essential authority figure. The sooner your child accepts this, the better off everyone will be.

Discipline from love. There are a number of practical ways to do this:

• Begin with a few important rules.
• Be very clear about what you expect from your child. You may need to explain things over and over, using lots of gestures.
• Speak slowly, not loudly. Your child is not hard of hearing.
• Tackle one major item at a time. Start with something essential such as getting your child's days and nights straightened out. This will be more difficult than you think but it has to be done for the sake of everyone involved, especially the child. It will help establish your authority.
• Find out as much as you can about child-rearing practices in your child's native country. They may be very different from ours. Any child will take some time to adjust. There may be a good reason why your child refuses to brush his teeth after every meal. He will come around in time.

If you have other children, they can be a big help in all this. Your newcomer is likely to take cues from them. If all children have to wash up for dinner, it won't be long before your new son or daughter routinely does so too. The same applies to bedtime, going to church, table manners, and a host of other details that make up daily family life.

Your other children can help their new brother or sister overcome fears of abandonment. For example, before Eileen went back to work after adopting Shanti, she and Shanti would take Raj to school every morning and pick him up after school. Shanti quickly understood that Mom dropped kids off and picked them up. She showed no fear the first morning Eileen left her at day care. She had learned that Eileen would be back.

## COMPLETING YOUR ADOPTION

When your child comes home, it may seem your adoption is complete but legally you have six months to a year to go. Most agencies will expect you to attend at least one postadoption counseling session. In addition, your social worker will pay at least one home visit to make sure that everything is going well. This visit is usually required by the courts. Your social worker will ask questions about your child and how you are adjusting to parenthood. This is an excellent opportunity to ask for help if you need it. Don't worry that you may lose the child if you express your feelings or ask for help with problems. Assuming that you aren't abusing or neglecting your child, no one wants to take anyone away. Your caseworker has a vested interest in helping you make your adoption work and will guide you toward the final adoption hearing.

You might not need to hire an attorney to complete the adoption. Check with the local court that handles adoptions (often a county court). Another parent can give you a copy of an adoption decree and you can retype it, changing the names and dates. Check with your local court officials about what supporting documents are needed and if yours are in the required form. If so, you will save several hundred dollars.

The final adoption hearing is a formality. It takes only a few minutes and should be a joyful experience. When you leave the courthouse, your child is yours, legally and forever. You now have the same responsibilities, rights, and privileges as any birth parent.

## NATURALIZATION

As soon as your child is formally adopted, he can become a U.S. citizen. Contact your regional Immigration and Naturalization Service office to apply.

The process is easy. The INS will give you forms spelling everything out. You will need to have a picture taken to meet strict specifications. Check the Yellow Pages for passport photographers. They have the equipment needed for naturalization photos.

Formerly, children receiving their citizenship were required to attend the swearing-in ceremony. Now attendance is optional. Depending on the age of your child, you may or may not want to attend the ceremony. It is very impressive, even moving, but it requires waiting in a courtroom for more than an hour. Federal judges are likely to speak at length about democracy and American heritage. Such speeches are splendid for adults and older children but won't mean anything to a two-year-old. However, even a small child is likely to enjoy the American flags and the refreshments at the reception after the ceremony.

If you make a party out of becoming a citizen, even a small child may have some memories of this very important occasion. If nothing else, they will enjoy the pictures. Eileen and Ron will never forget Raj's citizenship ceremony. He was an extremely energetic two-year-old with a very loud voice. Even several favorite books were not enough to keep him busy during the long wait for the ceremony to begin. Ron finally took him outside and barely made it back in time for the oath. Raj protested the whole time and was completely bored by the judge's eloquent speech on the Constitution. However, he loved the presents he received for becoming a citizen, attacked the sugar cubes at the reception, and treated his friends at day care to a Bert & Ernie cake. He has a hazy memory of the event and enjoys the stories of it.

## DISRUPTIONS

Even with counseling, some adoptions cannot be salvaged. Some parents wait until relationships have deteriorated so badly that they cannot be fixed. If this occurs after an adoption has been finalized, the original agency may never learn what has happened. The parents surrender the child to public authorities who find a foster home or other placement. If the disruption occurs before the adoption is finalized, the original caseworker usually finds another adoptive home for the child.

The veteran adoptive families often recruited for children with special needs or sibling groups are able to salvage many such adoptions. We know a family with eleven children, half adopted from various places with various problems. The children joke that you can't be a "real Brandt" unless you've had at least two previous parents.

The possibility of disruption should not deter prospective parents from adopting. The awareness that it can occur should encourage them to seek help if problems seem to be getting worse.

If your adoption agency is not helpful in counseling (or it is located halfway across the country), find a local counselor trained in working with "children in transition," those in foster care, adoption, or stepfamilies.

CHAPTER 9

# Raising an American
# Adopted from Overseas

No matter how American your child becomes—you, he, and other people will never forget that he was born somewhere else, especially if his race differs from yours. In chapter 4, we discussed some of the implications of this. In this chapter, we will look at rearing a foreign adopted child.

Some of the major issues you will cope with are common to any adoption, but your child's foreign origins may further complicate matters. On the other hand, you may face very little of what is presented here. So much depends on the individual child, as families with more than one child adopted from another country can attest.

## AN ADOPTIVE CHILDHOOD—WHO IS THIS CHILD?

To a certain extent, raising any child is like seeing a flower gradually open from a bud to full bloom. As experienced mothers, we know that all children are born with certain personality traits that seem to be "givens." With birth children, you may spot familiar "family signals" that provide you with a road map ("His temper is just like Uncle George's"). But even with birth children, these may be lacking.

With adopted children, you are denied these comfortable hereditary throwbacks and clues to behavior. You will have to learn to read the signals your child is sending. Is he outgoing or shy? Is he easygoing or stubborn? How does he relate to other children? Is he happy-go-lucky or serious? What kinds of activities does he most enjoy? What do these tell you about him? What seem to be his strengths and weaknesses? Does he catch on to things quickly or does he need a bit more time? Is he highly verbal? Is he a very physical child? Is he a bit of a roughneck or basically gentle? Can you see any patterns?

In a short time, you will have a handle on whom you are dealing with. Even though you cannot make the automatic analogies based on heredity that you might with a birth child, you may find that your child resembles some of your relatives. Spotting such similarities can be very helpful as you try to figure out who your child is and how he is likely to react to a given situation. .

It will help if you and your child are compatible. But there are no guarantees that you would be compatible with a birth child. Your birth daughter could just as well resemble great-aunt Ethel, the family's gossipy scold, as great-aunt Mary, who baked the world's best cinnamon rolls and invented wonderful games. Your adopted child may be a source of special joy and delight precisely *because* he or she doesn't have some family traits that you have never liked.

## INTRODUCING THE IDEA OF ADOPTION

One of the hardest but most important tasks of any adoptive parent is helping the child understand adoption. When the child is very young, it seems a little silly. Who can explain adoption to an eighteen-month-old?

As she gets older the right time may just never seem to come. The subject may seem threatening, awkward, or both. It's a little like discussing sex. It has to be done, but many parents would prefer to do it tomorrow. Other parents (like those who insist on talking endlessly about sex) feel it is imperative to fully explain everything about adoption to their children at a very early age. They may even introduce their child as "Jane, my adopted daughter." This is almost as bad as pretending Jane wasn't adopted because it makes adoption the center of her identity. She may even wonder if you fully accept her as your daughter.

We suggest that you treat adoption as a natural part of your family life and history without dwelling on it excessively. One good way is to show your child pictures of her arrival and tell "her" story from "her" book, with comments about how happy you were to get her. An older adopted child can participate in the family preparation for an adopted sibling or a friend's adoption. This is an excellent way to help your child understand what happened to her in a very happy context.

You should make adoption seem what it is—a joyful experience. Answer any questions, but keep the answers simple. You want to keep your child from developing the idea that being adopted is anything to feel inferior or insecure about. This is difficult in a society that still harbors pronounced biases against adoption. The key is your intense love for your child and her awareness that she is secure in that love.

## YOUR CHILD'S BIRTH IDENTITY: THE PUZZLE OF HIMSELF

We have already alluded to the fact that identity will be a continuing issue for your child. He will be curious about his original identity. This curiosity will include both his personal history and his cultural identity. He will be especially curious about how and why he came to be adopted. Unfortunately, you very likely will not have answers to many of his questions.

There is a bittersweet quality about adoptive love. While you may not want to think about your child's birth mother, you can never forget that she existed. When you talk about her with your child, show your respect and gratitude. Remember, your child will resent any slighting references to her. He probably has fantasies about her, especially when you have had a disagreement or he has had a hard day. From the age of five or six on, your child is likely to start asking questions such as:

- Why was I adopted?
- What happened to my mother?
- Where does she live now?
- Do I have brothers and sisters I don't know about?
- What does my mother look like?

Older children may speculate that they are related to people from their countries of origin whom they have read or heard

94

about. For example, Raj wondered if an Indian scientist who had invented a computerized way of duplicating handwriting could be his father. After all, Raj had had the same idea. Didn't this mean they could be related?

Unfortunately most foreign adoptees and their parents will never obtain information to answer any of the significant questions about family origins that children ask. In most cases, it isn't available. Neither is vital information that you might need, such as your child's family health history.

If you have a sensitive child, he is likely to say things that cause you pain because you know he is hurting—like commenting that he feels lonely because he really isn't related to anyone or because no one in the family looks like him. About all you can do is lend your child a very sympathetic ear. Encourage him to keep talking about his feelings. You can hope that the many good things in his life partially compensate for the loss of his birth identity—a central part of ourselves that most of us take for granted.

Be sensitive to the pain this causes. Let him know you understand why he wants answers. Above all, your child must know that you love him more than you could ever say and that he can always come to you with his fears and questions.

You will need to spend a lot of time with your child to be aware of what is going on and why. A lot of your best conversations will be while you're doing other things like baking cookies or taking a hike. If your child is willing to discuss difficult issues, it is a good indication that he feels secure.

## YOUR CHILD'S BIRTH IDENTITY:
## TWO CULTURES FOR DINNER

Several years ago, Americans of many backgrounds began looking for their roots. Spurred by the television series of that name, people began to explore what it meant to be Irish, Polish, African American, or Jewish.

Your child will probably experience this same desire in somewhat more intense fashion, especially when she begins to develop her own distinct identity in late childhood and early adolescence.

We strongly encourage you to recognize your child's distinct heritage by learning about it and displaying its symbols along with other family ethnic icons. You will need to walk a fine line between recognizing your child's distinct identity and making her feel like an outsider by pushing it down her throat. We suggest that you develop some consciousness of the ethnic roots of *all* family members so that discussion of your daughter's background is set in a context of enjoyment of differences. If Dad is Czech, serve kolaches in his honor one day and tandoori chicken for your daughter from India another day. Keep it light. Make it fun for everyone.

Try to establish a rapport with people from your child's country. Join a cultural group from your child's country or host a foreign student. Watch the newspaper for announcements of ethnic festivals or other events where your child may be exposed to the music, dancing, and art of her native land. Visit an ethnic grocery store. See if you can find a native costume.

Don't continue with any activity that you and your child don't enjoy. Your daughter will know if you're forcing yourself to do something just for her benefit. She may pretend to enjoy something just to please you. After sampling a new group or activity, talk about it and keep trying things until you find something that works.

Try to provide your child with proud images of her birth culture. For example, India is not just poverty-stricken millions living on the streets of Calcutta. It has a tremendously rich and varied culture, some of the world's finest art and architecture, Nobel prize winners, a fascinating history, and heroes such as Mahatma Gandhi and Nehru. There are world famous musicians such as sitar player Ravi Shankar and acclaimed film director Satyajat Ray, among many others.

Do not let your preteen child watch any television show where people from her country are depicted as starving masses. This will damage her self-image. As she grows older, she can develop a balanced understanding of her native country.

## RELATIONSHIPS WITH OTHER CHILDREN

Other children will be curious about your child's adoption. They will ask him where he is from and what happened to his "real mother." You will need to give him answers to these questions very early because they start in preschool or day care. Be calm and matter of fact. Children usually mean no harm, but they are curious and (by adult standards) tactless.

If you find your child is being regularly bullied because he is different, talk to school authorities. There may be a need for some cultural awareness training or even some stiff discipline. No child should have to face harassment because he is Asian or Latin American. On the other hand, don't get overly excited if your child complains about an occasional remark on the playground or says that no one likes him. When your child comes home with such a remark, test it against what you have seen of him with his friends. Is he truly shunned (because you never see him bring a friend home, get invited to a party or to play, or receive a phone call), or is he just having a bad day? Most parents who are tuned in to their children's lives can tell the difference.

If you think your child has a problem, contact his teacher or counselor, try to determine its cause, and work toward a solution. Many non-adopted children struggle with popularity problems too. Adoption per se may not even be an issue. Can the teacher suggest ways to help your child make friends? Is your child doing something that turns other children off? Is she shy? Is she aggressive?

Help your child develop confidence by encouraging her to get involved in activities at which she excels. No one makes fun of the softball team's best hitter for long. Activities are great for making friendships based on common interests. A child who has even one or two close friends will survive a few bullies without too many scars.

Think back to your own childhood. Were you popular? Did you have days when you felt like you didn't have a friend in the world? Were there parties you weren't invited to? How did you cope? Share these memories with your child. This alone can be very reassuring.

## WORKING WITH SCHOOLS

If you adopt an infant or toddler, you probably will have no more difficulty dealing with your school system than the average parent. If you adopt an older child, be prepared to be an advocate for your child.

Although most foreign adopted older children learn spoken English rapidly, it takes five to seven years for them to master academic English. By "academic English" we mean the vocabulary in which school instructions often are conveyed, especially on standardized tests. Your child may be perfectly able to communicate and still not understand seemingly simple directions such as "let's rhyme words."

Anyone who has ever tutored new English speakers learns very quickly how important context is to understanding the language. Most words have two or three meanings, which native speakers automatically sort out from context. New speakers don't have this advantage. No wonder they are often confused.

Unfortunately, this difficulty in mastering academic English causes some foreign-born children to be mislabeled as learning impaired or retarded. Such assessments are usually based on a combination of classroom performance and standardized tests. *Do not allow your child to be placed in a special-education class without further exploration of your child's abilities and needs.*

Fortunately, a federal civil-rights law requires school districts to provide all children with equal educational opportunity. If your district does not have an English as a Second Language program for non-native English speakers, it is required to provide the equivalent for your child. This may mean special tutoring.

Be prepared to insist on your rights. Your child's educational future may be at stake. If you know other parents who have the same problem, work together to ensure that your school district meets the needs of your children. Many school officials are not even aware of the needs of such children. They aren't familiar with the research on the lag in learning academic English because children tend to sound so good. They might be happy to help when they understand. They may also discover other children from non-English speaking backgrounds who need the help you are requesting.

## COPING WITH AWKWARD SCHOOL ASSIGNMENTS

As your child goes through school, you may wonder why sensitivity to adoption is not among our society's numerous other "sensitivities." Well-meaning teachers sometimes forget that not *all* youngsters have cute baby pictures to show off (especially pictures with Mom and Dad). They may not think how an adopted child feels about filling out a family tree. What is an adopted child to do when asked questions such as "How much did you weigh when you were born?" or "What time of day were you born?"

Sex education and family-life courses often overlook adoption. The adopted child may feel strange knowing she did not "grow in (her adoptive) Mommy's tummy" the way most other kids did. At a minimum, adoption should be recognized as a special, valid, and different means by which families are formed.

Adoptive parents (not just foreign adoptive parents) need to lobby their schools to be sensitive to the feelings and needs of adopted students. Examine your child's school family-life materials in advance so that you can tactfully address a problem before it arises. Many teachers would be happy to include adoption if only someone asked.

Contact your local intercultural family organization to see if it has materials on adoption (especially foreign adoption) that your school could use. Volunteer to serve on a parent curriculum committee or try to start one. Presume that you are dealing with people of goodwill who are merely thoughtless, not malicious. You may be surprised what you can accomplish.

## SOCIAL LIFE AND DATING

As your child gets older, his skin color may complicate his social life, especially when it comes to dating. The United States is still far from color-blind. Classmates who are happy to be friends with your foreign adopted child may shy away from dating him. Their parents may disapprove. They may fear that others will stare at them or make fun of them. This can be extremely painful for your child.

Ironically, your child may face special difficulty dating others from his nationality group. Some Asian-American parents may share their own nation's biases against adopted children.

Attractive Asian girls probably face the least social discrimination. Dark-skinned young persons of any nationality are likely to face greater problems if they want to date or marry whites. Minority teens may get very tired of being paired with each other at school functions.

Much of what happens depends on individual personalities. Extroverted, athletic, "popular" adopted teens will be better accepted than those who are quiet, awkward, and lacking in self-confidence. Doesn't that sound like all teenagers?

In general, your foreign adopted teen can be expected to face all the standard problems of the teenage years, with a few added complications due to skin color and the identity issues that are inescapable.

It may be hard for you to sort out which problems are standard adolescent difficulties and which are adoption-related. It may not even make any difference. What is most important is that you continue to make home a "safe" place for your child—a place where he knows he is loved and accepted and where he can express his hurts. Encourage your child to get involved in activities where he excels and where he will meet other young people with common interests.

## FIGHT YOUR OWN UNCERTAINTIES

You will cope a lot better with the special joys and difficulties of raising a foreign adopted child if you have worked through your own lingering questions about your legitimacy as an adoptive parent.

You may find your confidence being undermined in odd ways. The growing activism of birth mothers wanting to reunite with the children they placed for adoption certainly can cause some uncomfortable feelings. Who are you? Are you a parent or just a loving caretaker? If your child's birth mother came along, would you be cast off?

Whenever such thoughts occur, put them aside. They are counterproductive. You are the only *real* parents your child has. He or she was placed for adoption for good reasons. If you had not adopted your child, her future would have been far less promising.

It may help to think about a beautiful sermon that Eileen once heard. The priest's text was from one of the letters of the apostle Paul, where he refers to members of the Christian community as the "adopted children of God."

100

The priest then told the congregation about his adopted nephew and the great love his sister and her husband have for the boy. He talked about how much the boy resembles his dad and how close they are.

These parents and their adopted son teach us something about God's love, the priest said. Just as these adoptive parents are their son's *real* parents, so too are we God's adopted children, God's *real* children.

So also, thought Eileen, smiling broadly in her front pew with her two beautiful adopted children, have you just said something profound about the nature of adoptive love. Bless you, Father. Bless you.

CHAPTER 10

# Foreign Relations

Before Eileen went to Thailand, she knew that someone there had processed the papers she had sent, taken care of Shanti, and made arrangements with the Thai welfare officials for the approval of the adoption. But she had no idea who had, in effect, been representing her.

She had no direct contact with the Holt workers in Thailand until her trip to Bangkok. There she met a social worker named Pat who epitomizes the foreign half of the American-foreign partnership, which is critical to the success of any foreign adoption.

For five or six days, Pat, a tiny, hardworking, dedicated professional, was the key person in Ron and Eileen's lives. She was in charge of all their adoption-related activities. She seemed to know everybody connected with foreign adoption. If something went wrong or was delayed, she got matters back on track. She collected documents from government officials and guided families through processing at the American Embassy. She ensured that Shanti and another Holt adoptee were where they needed to be, and on time, although their foster homes were in outlying areas.

When Ron and Eileen were ready to leave Bangkok, Pat suggested an appropriate gift for Shanti's foster family, but refused any token of gratitude. Eileen, however, would never forget her kindness or the long hours she worked during their visit. Clearly this was a very dedicated young woman.

Ron and Eileen were not the only Americans who felt deep appreciation for her help. Two years later, Pat toured the United

States to see how adopted Thai children were faring. More than fifty people from Nebraska, Iowa, and South Dakota gathered for a dinner in her honor in Des Moines. She was obviously moved.

We discuss Pat's work at some length because it symbolizes the service of legions of foreign adoption workers and officials, without whom no foreign adoption would ever occur.

Sometimes Americans become impatient with the people and procedures they encounter in adopting abroad. They may feel helpless and insecure and resent the cultural differences.

As we detail the requirements of various countries (some of which may not please Americans hoping to adopt), we think it is extremely important to place foreign adoption in its intercultural context.

Americans have no right to adopt foreign children. It is a privilege granted by the countries of origin. These nations have every right to impose whatever restrictions they choose and to insist on whatever procedures they devise. Most foreign workers administering the systems are dedicated to protecting the children to be adopted. Their procedures are designed to contribute to that end. Many were instituted to combat abuses.

Social workers may be unfamiliar with the United States and unsure about the people who are adopting. They may find Americans and their ways as confusing and irritating as Americans find theirs. Americans who are insensitive to this viewpoint probably should reconsider foreign adoption—especially from a country that requires travel to pick up the child.

In this chapter we will discuss the "foreign relations" of adoption, including:

- Requirements of various countries
- Approximate costs by countries
- Relating to foreign adoption workers
- Appropriate donations to foreign adoption agencies
- Adoption flow chart: what happens when

## REQUIREMENTS BY COUNTRIES

The chart on page 105 gives the basic foreign adoption requirements for nine nations that are among the major sources of foreign adopted children. The countries we have listed (which are also profiled in chapter 19) are Colombia, Guatemala, Honduras, India, Korea, Nicaragua, Peru, the Philippines, and Thailand. If you are interested in another country, ask your social worker for equivalent information.

As you can see, rules vary considerably. You may be able to tell at a glance which countries might accept you. This will help you narrow your search for an agency to one working in one of these nations.

If you qualify for most countries, your choice may be dictated by the countries in which your agency works. If you are strongly attracted to a nation with which no local agency works, search nationwide for an adoption contact. Eileen and Ron did this successfully with India.

## EXPENSES BY COUNTRY

As we have stated in chapter 5, adoption expenses vary rather widely by country. Such costs are continually changing—and never going down. The following budgets are estimated ranges of what an adoption from each of the nine countries might cost as this book goes to press. These fees *do not* include home study costs or travel expenses.

### 1. COLOMBIA

Administration Fees..........................................$2,000 to $5,000
Attorney Fees/
    Foster Care (in some cases)..........................$6,000 to $8,000*
Dossier Fees.......................................................$500 to $600
Miscellaneous (embassy, passport,
    health check).................................................$1,000 to $1,500
Suggested Orphanage Donation
    (institutional children)...............................$1,000 to $3,000

---

*Not all Colombian adoptions involve use of a private attorney or fees for private foster care. Going through a government orphanage can reduce costs considerably, but the adoption may take longer and the child is likely to be older, not an infant.

| COUNTRY | COLOMBIA | GUATEMALA | HONDURAS | INDIA | KOREA | NICARAGUA | PERU | PHILIPPINES | THAILAND |
|---|---|---|---|---|---|---|---|---|---|
| PARENT AGE | APPROX.25 | 25 | 25 | 25-40 | 25-45 | 25 | MIN-30 | 25-40 | 30 |
| MARRIAGE LENGTH | 2 YEARS | 2 YEARS | 2 YEARS | 2 YEARS | 3 YEARS | | 2 YEARS | 3 YEARS | 5 UNLESS INFERTILE |
| DIVORCES | 1/SPOUSE | 1/SPOUSE | 1/SPOUSE | N/A | 1/SPOUSE | 1/SPOUSE | 1/SPOUSE | 1/SPOUSE | NONE |
| FAMILY INCOME | $20,000 | $20,000 | $20,000 | $20,000 | $25,000 | $20,000 | $20,000 | $20,000 | $30,000 |
| MAX # CHILDREN | N/A | N/A | N/A | N/A | 4 | N/A | N/A | N/A | 1 IF OF OPPOSITE SEX |
| SINGLE PARENTS | NO | YES | YES | NO | NO | YES | YES | SPCL NEEDS OVER 5 | NO |
| TRAVEL REQUIRED | YES | YES | YES | NO | NO | YES | YES | NO | YES |
| STAY REQUIRED | 2 WEEKS MIN. | 5-10 DAYS | 1 LONG OR 2 SHORT | N/A | N/A | 7-10 DAYS | 6-8 WEEKS OR 2 SHORT TRIPS | N/A | 7-10 DAYS |
| ADOPTION COMPLETE | COLOMBIA | GUATEMALA | HONDURAS | U.S. | U.S. | NICARAGUA | PERU | U.S. | U.S. |

## 2. GUATEMALA

Administration Fees ...........................................$2,000 to $5,000
Attorney Fees/Private
   Foster Care (some cases) ............................$3,000 to $8,000*
Suggested Donation to
   Orphanage (institutional children) ...........$1,000 to $3,000
Dossier Fees ....................................................$300 to $600
Miscellaneous .................................................$1,000 to $1,500

## 3. HONDURAS

Administration Fees ...........................................$2,000 to $5,000
Attorney Fees/
   Foster Care (some cases) ............................$5,000 to $8,000*
Dossier Fees ....................................................$300 to $600
Miscellaneous .................................................$2,000 to $2,500
Foster Care .....................................................$250 per month
between the two trips

## 4. INDIA

Administration Fees ...........................................$2,000 to $8,000
Attorney Fees ..................................................$1,000
Dossier Fees ....................................................$300 to $500
Miscellaneous ..................................................$500
Orphanage Donation Suggested

## 5. KOREA

Administration Fees ...........................................$5,000 to $6,000
Escort Fee to U.S. .............................................$2,000

## 6. NICARAGUA

Administration Fees ...........................................$2,000 to $2,500
Attorney Fees ..................................................$200
Dossier Fees ....................................................$300 to $500
Miscellaneous .................................................$1,000 to $1,500
Orphanage Donation Suggested

*See note on Colombia.

## 7. PERU

Administration Fees .........................................$2,000 to $7,000
Attorney Facilitation Fees/
   Private Foster Care...................................$8,000 to $10,000*
Dossier Fees ............................................................$300 to $500
Miscellaneous..................................................$1,000 to $1,500
Donation to Orphanage Suggested
   for Institutional Cases

## 8. PHILIPPINES

Administration Fees ........................................$2,000 to $9,000
Dossier Fees ............................................................$300 to $600
Miscellaneous.....................................................................$500

## 9. THAILAND

Administration Fees .......................................$2,000 to $6,000
Dossier Fees ............................................................$500 to $800
Miscellaneous.....................................................................$500
Orphanage Donation Suggested
   (or gift to foster family)

The tremendous range in fees for various categories and various countries is due to the differing programs placing children. Clearly, in some countries it is more expensive to work through a private attorney than an orphanage. Reputable adoption agencies carefully screen participating attorneys, but attorney-assisted adoptions are simply more expensive.

Discuss various options with your social worker and together develop a plan that works for you and is within your budget.

## RELATING TO FOREIGN ADOPTION WORKERS

If you go to the foreign country to bring home your child, it will be very important to establish a good relationship with the foreign adoption workers who will be helping you. As you have already

*See note on Colombia.

learned from your dealings with adoption workers in the United States, you are dependent on their goodwill.

We suggest the following guidelines:

- No one has ever improved on the Golden Rule. Do unto the social workers as you would have them do unto you.
- Remember, you are a guest in a foreign country, which is doing you an enormous favor by permitting you to adopt. Show your respect and gratitude.
- Don't complain about how things are done in the foreign country or compare the nation unfavorably to the U.S.
- Be patient but persistent. Keep asking for what you need but do so pleasantly.
- Don't embarrass your social worker by trying to use political clout or by going over her head to someone higher in the agency.
- Don't be surprised if some things take longer than in the U.S. Most social welfare offices in the countries from which children come aren't automated. It takes longer to do things by hand.
- Remember that your adoption is a low priority for most of the foreign governments. Many are struggling to meet the needs of their own citizens, and have scarce resources to devote to foreigners.
- If you have any questions about the legality or propriety of some things that might be suggested by some people you meet, check with your American social agency or the American Embassy. Don't take risks that can jeopardize your adoption and that of many other people.
- Show your gratitude by making a donation to the orphanage where your child has stayed. Such orphanages tend to be desperately poor and rely heavily on donations. A social worker may discreetly suggest the customary amount. If she doesn't, ask. While donations may not be *required*, if they are customary, treat them as an obligation.
- While your social workers or their agencies may be unable to accept any kind of gratuity, make a gracious gesture of thanks such as sending flowers or taking them to lunch.

- When you return, you *must* send pictures showing your child in his new home. Many workers grow attached to the children and mourn their departure. Pictures showing how happy your child is help ease the pain and promote good adoption relations. You might send a note and a picture about once a year for several years.

## TIMETABLE

The following is an approximate timetable that most foreign adoptions follow. We have suggested the major activities that might occur during the six-month intervals of an adoption taking two years or less. Individual adoptions may vary considerably. Some will take less than a year, others more than two years, depending on the country and individual circumstances. However, this should give you an idea about what happens during the course of a typical adoption.

One to six months
- Gather adoption information
- Attend information meetings
- Select agency
- Complete home study
- Prepare dossier
- File preliminary I-600A

Six to twelve months
- Complete any remaining details on dossier
- Prepare culturally
- WAIT
- Possible child assignment
- Agency sends dossier
- Possible completion of I-600A
- Possible arrival of escorted children

Twelve to eighteen months
- Possible child assignment
- Possible completion of I-600A
- Possible first trip or only trip to foreign country

- Possible arrival of child
- Possible finalization of adoption

Eighteen to twenty-four months
- Child arrival
- Second trip if necessary
- Possible finalization of adoption
- Possible naturalization

## SUMMARY

Foreign adoption is a complicated process, but every year at least eight thousand Americans succeed in bringing children into the United States. We have tried to outline the major issues, barriers, problems, and costs you will face.

If it sounds a little overwhelming, don't be deterred. It all moves step by step. Your agency will guide you through what you must do, and you have ample time to do it.

Above all else, you are not alone. With minimal effort, you can find veteran adoptive families to help you, in addition to your social workers.

While it is not necessary to be religious to adopt, those who have a faith of some sort will find it a great source of comfort and strength. Both of us were aided during the long months of our adoptions by a strong sense that God was using this process to accomplish something very wonderful for the children and for our families.

# CHAPTER 11

# Adoption Miracles

*"God makes adoptions. We just do the paperwork."*

Every adoption story is its own small miracle. Almost any adoptive parent will recount the coincidences that, in retrospect, seemed to fall so neatly into place: the phone call that came on just the right day, the chance conversation with a relative or friend that led to a referral, the complete stranger who played a key role.

Undoubtedly there are good atheists who still don't believe in God after they get their children, but even they must catch themselves praying their way through some of the tenser moments! Many adoptive parents feel the power of God more intensely than at any other time in their lives. They sense that God is arranging things for them and their children in a way that transcends human logic and power.

Here are three of Joan's favorite adoption "miracle" stories, when it seemed that God was working overtime.

## 1. THE TWINS

Soon after Holt's Nebraska office opened, Joan met a mother, a former Minnesotan, who had adopted an eighteen-month-old Korean girl through an agency in Minnesota. The mother, who was president of the local intercultural families group, wanted to adopt a six-year-old Korean girl she had heard about. Joan wasn't sure that the six-year-old was the right child for them.

However, after a meeting one day, the mother, whom we will call Ann Anderson, asked to look at the six-year-old's picture. Joan said sure. They chatted as Joan sorted through a stack of papers to find the picture. Finally she found it and gave it to Ann. Stuck under it was a picture of an eighteen-month-old Korean girl, which fell to the floor. Ann picked it up, glanced at it casually and said "This little girl looks just like Susan" (her Korean daughter).

Meanwhile Joan and Ann continued talking about the six-year-old. Joan tried to put the picture of the eighteen-month-old away, but again it fell to the floor. Ann picked it up and looked at it again.

When she left, she said, "Can I take this picture and show it to my husband? This little girl looks so much like Susan." Joan agreed.

That night, when Joan came home about 11:30 P.M., she found a huge message scrawled on shelf paper, which went all the way around the kitchen: "Mom, call Ann Anderson no matter what time you get home." Joan called and found Ann almost breathless with excitement.

"They're twins," Ann said. "I know they're twins. I've checked her name, K-number, date of birth, and birthplace with Susan's and they're the same. Listen to this. This little girl's adoption number and Susan's are consecutive. I know that siblings are always listed that way."

To Joan's astonishment, Ann was right. Further checking with Holt's Oregon headquarters resolved the mystery. Susan Anderson was born healthy and immediately placed for adoption through the Minnesota agency. Her twin was born with cerebral palsy and held in Korea. Later, the twin was placed for adoption through Holt and her picture came to Joan. If Ann hadn't moved to Nebraska, met Joan and accidentally seen the picture, she would never have discovered that Susan had a twin.

When Joan called Oregon, Holt staff members had just assigned the twin to a family on the East Coast. Joan begged the worker to pull the placement. He said it was already in the mail. Then he thought twice. Because it was very early in the morning when Joan called, the mail might not have gone out yet. The staff member ran to the mail room, pulled the letter to the East

112

Coast family out of a mailbag and changed the assignment to the Andersons.

A few months later, Sally arrived in Nebraska to begin her new life with her twin sister and new parents.

## 2. MATCHING HANDICAPS

Twila and her husband, Dwayne Westercamp, are remarkable people, the kind who always turn problems into opportunities. Twila, a cheerful, brave soul, had suffered a stroke, which totally disabled her left side. Dwayne is a talented handyman. After Twila's stroke, he modified their home to allow Twila to cope with her problem. Twila learned to do everything one-handed. She cooked, cleaned, took care of her family and herself. She lived a full life.

Both she and Dwayne wanted a large family. Five years after their first child, Matt, was born, they adopted Nicole, a Korean baby. That worked out extremely well. Four years later, they applied for another child. They wanted another girl from any country.

Soon after Joan completed their home study update, the Westercamps became close friends with another family, who were adopting through KESIL. While both couples were waiting for their referrals, Joan received word of a Korean boy with special needs who was to be placed with the Westercamps' friends.

When Twila heard about the child, however, she informed Joan that "this is our child." She had good reason to request the boy. He had been born with an enlarged left arm, which he was expected to lose eventually. Twila and Dwayne felt they were especially qualified to raise him. Their friends agreed to wait for another child.

Soon after Twila and Dwayne accepted the boy, they learned that his arm would have to be removed because of cancer. They urgently moved to bring him to the United States for surgery. Papers were hand-carried to various agencies in Korea for approval. Within days, instead of the usual three months, Ben was en route to Omaha for surgery. Doctors said the normal three-month wait could have cost him his life.

Ben recovered and adjusted to life within his new home—already conveniently modified for a boy with an artificial left

113

arm. More important, he had found parents who seemed made just for him.

## 3. FROM GUATEMALA TO IOWA

The first time Joan went to Guatemala to arrange an adoption, she stayed with missionaries outside Guatemala City. One day when she had to pick up an immigration packet at the American Embassy there, the missionaries dropped her off and told her where to meet them. They said they would be back in an hour. They were adamant as to where she was to stand. They said the crowds were so great elsewhere that they wouldn't be able to find her. However, when Joan left the Embassy, an American guard pushed her out of the way and said the area was off limits.

Unable to speak Spanish and afraid that the missionaries would never find her, Joan asked God a direct question: "What am I supposed to do now?"

Another short woman who was also standing and waiting supplied the answer. The woman looked American.

"Are you an American?" Joan asked, almost desperately.

"Yes," she replied.

"What are you doing here?" asked Joan.

"I'm Flo Martin from Texas," the woman explained. "My husband and I run an orphanage at Quesaltananga up in the mountains four hours drive from here. I'm here to help some folks adopt a baby."

"I'm here to find out about adoptions from Guatemala myself," Joan replied. "Can I come see your orphanage?"

"Perhaps next week," Flo answered. Because Joan was leaving the next day, she couldn't make it. However, they exchanged addresses and phone numbers. Joan made a mental note to try to look Flo up if she ever returned to Guatemala. When her missionary friends found her, Joan shoved Flo's address and phone number in the back of her billfold and went on to other matters.

Joan never forgot Flo, but she had no further contact with her for four years. Then one day, a couple from Iowa called Joan and pleaded with her to do a home study. They wanted to adopt a child in an orphanage in Guatemala but couldn't find anyone to do the home study, because the child had been located through

114

missionaries—not an adoption agency. When Joan asked more questions, she learned that the child was in a remote area four hours from Guatemala City. Could the child possibly be in Flo's orphanage?

"Is this orphanage in Quesaltananga? Are you working with the Martins?" Joan asked.

"Yes," said the wife in surprise. "How could you possibly know them?"

"I met her on a street corner in Guatemala City," said Joan. "I'd be delighted to help you."

Several months later, the Iowans went to Guatemala to adopt their son. As a result of Joan's "chance" street-corner meeting with Flo, a number of children from Guatemala have found homes in the United States.

## POSTSCRIPT

These stories aren't exactly typical, but they illustrate the special beauty of adopting from another country. Almost every parent who has adopted a child from another country can think of at least one small miracle connected with his or her adoption experience. It may help to think of these examples when you are going through the process and are encountering a special period of difficulty or delay.

CHAPTER 12

# A Single Parent Adopts

About a week before Thanksgiving 1984, Cathy Beck of Omaha stunned relatives attending a family gathering with an announcement: "I'm expecting a child."

A hush fell over the room and all eyes turned to Cathy—single, thirty-two, and devoutly Catholic. Hastily she amended her statement: "I mean I've put in for adoption."

There was some surprise, much rejoicing, and a few concerns when Cathy said she would have to go to Central America to get her child. But a year later, Cathy was the mother of a beautiful baby girl, Katie, born in Honduras on the day she first contacted the adoption agency.

"I had always wanted to become a parent," Cathy recalled. "I was always told I would make a great mom. When I decided to adopt I was thirty-two, not married, and not dating anyone. I saw no potential of having kids. The only route open to me, given my religion, was adoption."

Cathy first explored domestic adoption and found the doors closed. Then she looked into foreign adoption and "nothing seemed to be terribly open there either." So she went on with her life. She continued working in the business she owns and bought a house. Although options seemed closed, the dream would not die. In September 1984, a series of articles in the local newspaper about homeless children in Brazil changed her life.

One story profiled a local single woman who had adopted two daughters from South America. Cathy clipped the story and carried it around for a week. Finally she called the woman. They talked for two hours.

"She (the woman) told me to call Joan (Worden)," Cathy said. "On Monday, the day Katie was born, I called Joan to start the process. She was terribly encouraging." Joan, who was running Holt International Children's Services' Nebraska office at the time, was impressed with Cathy's maturity and intense desire to adopt.

Although Holt had not previously placed children with single parents, Joan sensed that Cathy might be the woman to break that barrier, especially if she was willing to help Holt start a new program in Honduras.

In January 1985, Joan did Cathy's home study and asked if she would be willing to spend up to three months in Honduras. Cathy agreed.

"I had my own business and I could get away," she said. Cathy quickly filled out all the necessary papers, which were taken to Honduras almost immediately by a Holt staff member. Cathy then left for a brief ski trip because Joan had told her she would hear nothing for at least a week. The day after she arrived in Colorado, she received an emergency message to call home. Had something dreadful happened to her parents or family? Her brother answered the phone in a cheerful voice. Cathy breathed a sigh of relief.

"What's going on?"

"Not much," he replied.

"What the hell am I calling for?"

"Oh," he responded offhandedly. "You have a baby girl."

Cathy was frantic for details, but her brother had none. A call to Joan cut short her ski trip. It was then that she realized that her daughter, whom she had decided to name Katie, had been born on the day she had first called Joan. It seemed providential.

The next ten weeks were a madhouse as Cathy struggled to complete all the required paperwork and get documents approved. She left for Honduras after a hairbreadth episode at Chicago's O'Hare Airport. She had encountered typical bureaucratic delays getting the Honduran Consulate in Chicago to approve her adoption dossier. Among other documents, the consulate was holding her passport. The day before her departure, the consulate approved her papers. Cathy hired a messenger service to meet her at O'Hare and deliver the documents during a twenty-minute stopover. If she missed her plane, she would be unable to notify the orphanage in Honduras because it had no phone.

When Cathy's flight landed, she frantically asked for directions to United Parcel pickup where the messenger had said he would wait. No one knew where it was. Then she spotted a man carrying an envelope. He asked if she were Cathy Beck. "I grabbed the envelope and ran for the plane," she said.

Cathy was headed for the adventure of her life—six difficult weeks in a land where she knew no one and had to adjust to motherhood without the companionship and assistance of a spouse.

She met Katie soon after her arrival. Katie was beautiful and healthy with huge, dark eyes. Cathy was determined to do whatever it took to bring her home. She also met her lawyer and took custody of Katie, who had been living in an orphanage. During the six long, lonely weeks it took to finalize the adoption, Cathy and Katie stayed with an American teacher, a friend of a returned Peace Corps volunteer from Omaha.

"There was no radio or TV," Cathy said. "I had an infant so I hand washed cloth diapers, which I had brought with me. We went for walks a lot. I lost twelve pounds. I kept checking on how things were coming with my papers. There were times when a whole week would go by and I wouldn't make a phone call. I bugged them when it seemed appropriate."

Cathy read books she had brought, called home weekly and wrote letters. The highlight of her day was the arrival of the mail. "Letters were like nutrition to me, like chocolate. I would read letters over and over until the next one came. I was bored a lot. Time moved terribly slowly. It would seem like two hours had passed and ten minutes had gone by."

Finally Cathy's case went to court. Her lawyer, whom she had found through Holt, questioned the birth mother. "It was pretty bad," Cathy said. "I almost thought she wouldn't do it."

A social worker filled out all the required forms and submitted them to the wife of the president of Honduras, who was in charge of adoption. This caused a week's delay. "I talked to her aides three times a day for a week," Cathy said. Finally the papers were signed.

Katie was then issued a new birth certificate and passport, went to a doctor who had to stamp the passport, then to the American consulate for final processing. At last Cathy could take Katie home to begin their new life. That new life proved to be satisfying, but very demanding for Cathy.

"There's no one to share parenting with or to give you a break. When you need a break is when you can least ask for it because you don't want to bother anyone," Cathy said. "Crises are not scheduled. You do what you need to do. You don't think what you would do if you had a husband."

Cathy said that when Katie was small, she would long for the relief of even a short walk alone or a solo trip to the grocery store to recover her equilibrium if Katie had been sick or crying. Such small, unscheduled breaks from parenting when a spouse can take over are denied a single parent.

However, Cathy made the adjustment so successfully that she has adopted a second Honduran baby girl after an even more difficult bureaucratic struggle.

As for the first adoption, Katie is beautiful and healthy. From the first, Cathy's family "adored her." Still, Katie notices that she doesn't have a father and many other children do.

"She would like a daddy because at school, she is with other children who have daddies," Cathy said. "Up to age four, this was not an issue. Once in awhile when she gets tired and is struggling to go to sleep, she has cried for her mom and dad in Honduras." Cathy said she is "not threatened" by such episodes. "Ninety percent of it is from fatigue."

Cathy said single people considering adoption need to be aware of several realities they will face:

- You lose your personal life. You are tied to that child. Sometimes you need to get out.
- If you are a party person and don't want to give that up, don't adopt.
- Think about how much this will cost. Babysitting alone is at least $250 a month. Foreign adoption expenses can be hard for a single person.
- Get a support system to help make up for the lack of a spouse. You will need it for everything from scheduling problems to emotional support.
- Your child will need friends. In a single-child, one-parent household, you are that child's playmate.

- Before adopting, think of your long-range plans. It might be cheaper to get a sibling group or to adopt a second child close in age at the same time.

Cathy recommended that single parents attend workshops on problems such as discipline to get the perspective of other parents. Cathy participates in a parent self-help group. She said she tries to concentrate on the realities she must face rather than what might be ideal.

"Income is tough and tight, but somehow the Lord is with me," she said. "Since I own my own business, I sweat it out when times are tough. I save every penny I can get my hands on for the tough times."

## SINGLE PARENT ADOPTIONS: JOAN'S PERSPECTIVE

Single people who wish to adopt will face much greater scrutiny than their married peers, but they can succeed if they are determined and well qualified.

Single parents have fewer foreign adoption options than couples. They are generally limited to nations in Central and South America.

Single people must meet the same criteria as married couples. In addition, social workers are likely to look closely at the following factors:

- Flexibility in employment: Does the prospective parent have enough flexibility to make arrangements to care for a sick child? Sometimes employers are cooperative when the situation is explained.
- Financial stability: Does the parent earn enough to support a child?
- Support system: Does the parent have relatives, friends, or neighbors who can provide assistance if needed? This is vital for single parents.

Single parents may actually be better than married people for some children, such as older children or children who have been abused or neglected. Such children are likely to form a strong bond with only one parent and may do better if they have to deal with only one person.

Prospective single parents may face greater sacrifices than their married peers because there is no one with whom to share responsibility. For example, if their current job requires considerable travel, they might need to change jobs. They probably also will have to give up more outside activities or substitute activities in which the child can become involved.

Some single parents worry that they may be depriving a child of the opportunity to have two parents. This should not be a consideration. The single parent is giving her adopted foreign child an opportunity to be educated and have a future that otherwise would be unavailable. She should concentrate on real issues such as how she will create a home for her child and a support system for herself.

Some single people believe that it will be easier to take care of an older child. This is unlikely to be true. While an older child will require less physical care than an infant, other problems will very likely be greater. Older children may suffer the effects of physical, emotional, and educational deprivation. They are more likely to have been abused. They may find it more difficult than a younger child to bond with a new parent. They may find it harder to make American friends or to fit in at school.

Even with the difficulties, some single parents may still prefer to adopt an older child. They may be especially skilled in coping with the problems. This is fine as long as they are under no illusions about what they may face or their ability to meet their child's needs.

## POSTSCRIPT

One of the beauties of today's international adoption scene is that it *is* open to qualified single people. They may have to work harder to find an agency that will work with them but as Cathy's story shows, it can be done. We encourage single people to explore their options in the same fashion a married couple would, and if their hearts tell them to adopt, to follow that inclination.

CHAPTER 13

# Adopting from Eastern Europe

It is little short of astonishing when we think about it. For years, adopting a child from another country has meant adopting from Asia or Latin America. Now, however, there's a new and rather volatile source of children: Eastern Europe.

We write this chapter in 1992 with some trepidation, knowing that nearly everything we write risks becoming dated even as we write it. Yet no book on the subject of foreign adoption should appear without at least some information on this topic. In this chapter we will:

- Discuss briefly what seems to be happening in the region.
- Look at what a couple might experience in attempting to adopt from Eastern Europe.
- Offer cautions and advice as to how to proceed.

## ADOPTION IN EASTERN EUROPE

When Communism fell in Romania, one of the most shocking discoveries was the existence of thousands of children languishing in orphanages. Many of them had been sadly neglected and had various health problems. The new government, however, opened the nation to international adoption, and large numbers of prospective adoptive parents from the United States and Western Europe either went to Romania or attempted to adopt through agencies at home. There were widespread allegations of baby selling and other unsavory practices. The Romanian government realized that it had to regulate international adoption. It effectively brought activity to a standstill while it established procedures and designated agencies with which it would work.

As of this writing, very few children are coming from Romania, but that could change. If you are interested in Romanian adoption, talk to your social worker and see what she can tell you about its current status. She may be able to refer you to an agency that is working in Romania or to assist you with other options in Eastern Europe.

Other countries that have opened their doors, at least in small measure, to international adoption since the fall of Communism include Bulgaria, Russia, Hungary, and Poland. We suggest that you explore these countries as well as Romania. For example, KESIL has already placed children from Bulgaria. We stress that the situation is fluid, and we cannot give specific information as we can with countries where international adoption is well established and regulated. Our strongest advice, as always, is to work cooperatively with a licensed, international agency rather than trying to find an attorney or a missionary to help you. You take great risks if you use that approach. Do not try to locate a child on your own.

## THE EASTERN EUROPEAN ADOPTION EXPERIENCE

By adopting from Eastern Europe, parents may believe that their children will be less "foreign" in appearance than those adopted from Asia or Latin America. Such parents may be disillusioned when they encounter the reality of Eastern European adoption. As Americans are becoming increasingly aware, the nations of Eastern Europe are not wealthy. Budgets for all needs, including those of children, are limited. In addition, children may not look like your expectations, since about half are from Gypsy families and have dark skin and eyes. These children resemble those from Latin America far more than they do stereotypical light-skinned Slavic children.

Many children who have been in crowded orphanages may need a great deal of special attention to overcome the impact of years of institutionalization. Workers in the institutions, by and large, are loving, hardworking, and nurturing people. But there

123

are many children, small staffs, and low budgets. They have done remarkably well with what they have. The children are clean and the orphanages are spotless.

Still, children in such settings cannot receive the personal attention and love that only families can supply. They may have difficulty trusting or forming attachments. Prospective parents will need to have flexible schedules to be able to spend large amounts of time giving their new children love and a sense of security. This may mean hours of just sitting and holding a child. Husbands and wives who both have demanding careers probably should not consider Eastern European adoption. The parenting requirements can approach those of children with special needs or handicapping conditions.

There may also be health problems. Families considering Eastern European adoption should have good medical insurance. Their children may arrive with conditions that have not been diagnosed. Common medical problems include hepatitis B and parasites.

In short, if you're trying to adopt the perfect white baby that you couldn't get without years of waiting in the United States, you should think twice about what may happen. You *could* end up adopting such a child, but you might not.

## PROCEDURES

Because international adoption work is so new to Eastern Europe, it changes constantly. A few patterns, however, are beginning to emerge:

- Other countries in the region have learned from Romania's experience and are taking a more cautious approach to allowing foreigners to adopt. They want to avoid a repeat of the scandals that led to Romania's new rules. In most Eastern European countries, adoptable children are first offered to citizens of those nations. If a child cannot be placed, he may be eligible for international adoption.
- Because international adoption is so new to them, government officials and orphanage directors in those nations may be confused about the process. They may inadvertently give

erroneous information to American adoption workers. Thus what your American caseworker tells you may turn out to be untrue through no one's fault. Be aware of the constant need to recheck and clarify every step of the process.

- Adoptive parents will have a more active role in the adoptive process. In many cases they will have to go to the country where assistance with procedures such as immigration completion may be minimal. They may have to make all travel arrangements without assistance and may have to find and hire an interpreter. Even if the country does not require both parents to travel to pick up the child, it is a good idea for both to go. They will need the support that spouses can give each other. They should both meet their prospective child at the same time.

- Costs will vary widely, especially as currencies fluctuate and the economies of the nations change. You may have to take cash to pay for adoption expenses. Traveler's checks, personal checks, and credit cards may not be acceptable. We suggest that you carry no bills larger than $20.00. Larger bills often cannot be changed. Again, you must discuss such matters in detail with your social worker.

## OUR ADVICE

Adoption from Eastern Europe is growing rapidly and will continue to grow. Within a few years, it will be as common as adoption from Korea once was. By that time, there should be well-established channels and procedures. Families who adopt from Eastern Europe now are the groundbreakers. They are taking the risks and experiencing the problems that arise in any new adoption program.

We don't want to discourage anyone who is willing to be a pioneer. We simply want to encourage pioneers to be realistic about life on the frontier and as informed as possible about what they may expect. This is *not* for parents who get upset when things don't work out exactly the way the social worker initially described. It can, however, be a wonderful and enriching way to build an adoptive family. We've seen a number of happy experiences already, and those numbers will multiply rapidly in the years to come.

CHAPTER 14

# Encountering Your Child's Birth Heritage

Eileen will never forget the night. Raj was nine and he had gotten in trouble at school—nothing earthshaking, but enough for Eileen to feel it was time for a mother-son talk. The talk was difficult. Eileen sensed that something important, but unspoken, lay behind the problem at school. The two sat in the dark in silence for some time. Then Raj began weeping for the birth mother he had never met.

Tears stung Eileen's eyes. This was not a ploy for sympathy. She could empathize with his desire to know more about his identity. Hadn't she spent a year obsessively exploring her Irish roots?

It's a scene that many adoptive parents have experienced with their children. No matter how much adoptive parents and children love each other, part of the child's identity is missing. Some feel it more acutely than others.

Now some Korean adoptees and their families may find at least partial answers to their questions. Joan and her agency Kids Each Served in Love (KESIL) can help Korean adoptees reunite with their birth families, or at least uncover some missing details in their life stories. The Korean Social Service Agency has selected KESIL as one of the American agencies to contact if adoptees want information about their birth families or to try to find their birth relatives.

It works like this. Adoptees or their parents should write to KESIL, P.O. Box 12175, Omaha, NE 68112 requesting that a search be made for their families. They should include as much information as possible:

- Their case number
- The name of the Korean agency that placed them
- A copy of their social history
- Their birth name
- The district from which they were placed

While there are no guarantees, the Korean Social Service Agency (one of the nation's four major adoption agencies) has promised to investigate all requests—no matter which agency placed the adoptee. Even adoptees who were abandoned may be able to learn something of their origins. The Korean Social Service Agency will examine old police and hospital records in the cities where the abandonments occurred on the dates when they were reported.

Until now, only cursory background checks have been made, providing little information that adoptees didn't already have. The agency believes that it may be able to find many birth parents or at least foster parents who might remember the children.

When families are located, the agency will see whether they have any interest in a reunion or will supply requested health information. If there is a mutual desire for a reunion, KESIL will organize family reunion tours.

Joan said that requests for reunions sent to KESIL will go in the permanent Korean adoption files. Even if the Korean Social Service Agency can't immediately locate a family, the presence of such a request could precipitate a reunion. She urges all parents to keep a note in their children's adoption files (if such files are kept in the country of origin) indicating a willingness to hear from the birth parent if the adoptive parents think their child might be interested in such a reunion someday.

Some Korean families are starting to seek information on the children they relinquished, as Joan's daughter Jodi's family did. The longstanding note that Joan had left in Jodi's file enabled her birth family to find her.

Even if parents cannot be located, adoptees may learn more of their life stories than they currently know. They may discover they had siblings who were also abandoned or relinquished and put up for adoption. It might be possible to locate some or all of these relatives.

Like all reunions between adopted children and their birth families, there are dangers. Adoptees may discover painful information about their life histories or their relatives. They may find that their birth families have no desire to see them. They may find that their adoptive families are threatened by their desire to search.

The reunions should be preceded and followed by intensive counseling for both adoptees and adoptive parents. A great deal of preparation is required for what is certain to be an extremely emotional encounter.

Joan was not prepared for the impact of Jodi's reunion with her birth family even though she was thrilled that it occurred. It was far more threatening than Joan would have imagined. It made her feel, at least for a time, like an outsider whose ties to her daughter were in danger.

"The first day of the reunion, Jodi's birth mother said that for the first time since giving her daughter up, she no longer had a knot in her stomach," Joan recalled. "I thought, yeah, sure. You've transferred it to me."

But those resentments softened as Jodi realized some of what Joan was feeling and included her in activities with her Korean family. Jodi filmed a touching moment where both mothers came out of a temple holding hands.

Jodi said she left Korea feeling like a whole person for the first time in her life. The experience strengthened her love for both her mothers and healed the pain of being sent away from her Korean family at age eight. Not all reunions would end so well, Joan said.

Jodi's family gave her up for adoption because they were economically desperate. They felt it was the loving thing to do—and they had never stopped loving Jodi. Today they are prosperous, proud, and happy. They took an enormous risk of losing face in trying to reunite with the daughter they could not forget.

However, some birth mothers might be horrified if their American children ever located them. Perhaps they were young and unmarried. Perhaps their husbands and children know nothing about a child placed for adoption years before. Perhaps there was scandal connected with the birth. An adopted child might be appalled to discover that his birth mother was raped or that she is a prostitute. He might be deeply hurt if he located his birth mother and she refused to see him.

128

One mother of a child whose adoption papers included a last name did a bit of detective work with friends from that nation. The name, they said, is a prominent one. It is likely that the birth mother placed her baby for foreign adoption to avoid the embarrassment of ever seeing him again. The mother suspects that an eventual search for a birth family could be successful, but would probably be unwise. The mother hopes her son never becomes terribly interested in searching, but recognizes that if he does, there will be little she can do to protect him.

Not all adopted children *do* wish to search for their birth parents, even if they think they could find them. Joan's other Korean daughter, Mindy, for example, has no interest in reuniting with her birth family. She never has had such an interest and Joan doesn't expect her to develop one. For her, that book closed many years ago. She has no desire to reopen it.

But for those who do, the KESIL-Korean Social Service Agency Reunion Program could mean the dream of a lifetime come true. Like Jodi, your foreign adopted child may finally come to terms with the identity questions that haunt her. Like Jodi, she may finally make peace with what happened to her and why it happened.

## OTHER COUNTRIES

Unlike Korea, many countries that send children to the United States maintain only sketchy birth or abandonment records.

Eileen and Ron, for example, were told that Raj had been baptized at Mother Teresa's orphanage in Delhi. When they requested a baptismal certificate or at least a date of baptism, they received a polite letter saying that different sisters had been transferred to the orphanage. No one could recall anything about Raj. There were no documents.

If there are no documents, searching will be futile. For many children, the identity issue will remain a lifelong question. There are, however, things adoptive parents can do to partially satisfy their children's curiosity about their origins. Parents adopting from Latin American countries, Eastern Europe, and Thailand are required to go there to get the children. There are enormous benefits in terms of the ability to help the child understand who he is and where he came from. Some Latin American countries require the birth mother to attend the court adoption proceeding. The adoptive parents meet her, uncomfortable though this may be. In later years, they can at least describe the woman to their children.

Adoptive parents gain priceless memories to share with their children:

- I saw the orphanage where you lived.
- I met the kind sisters who took care of you.
- I visited your house in Bangkok.
- Here are pictures of the city where you were born.
- Daddy and I bought you this necklace when we came to get you.
- I remember how hot it was the day we first met you.
- We went shopping together in the big central market. You had never before had ice cream.
- We were all so tired when we got off the plane after flying for twenty hours.

Parents who have been to the countries where their children were born gain a deeper sense of their children's identity. When your child is old enough, consider taking him on a trip to his native country. Even if he can't find any relatives, he'll gain a better sense of his heritage.

What's the right age to make such a trip? It varies with the child and the country. Some nations might be too uncomfortable or upsetting for children younger than eleven or twelve to understand and enjoy. Your child should be old enough to remember the trip.

Teenagers might be excited by such a trip or totally uninterested in it. They may be trying very hard to be just like all their friends. You'll have to judge what might work best for your child.

If you do plan a trip, try to make it a personal pilgrimage. Try to visit at least one site (a house, an orphanage, or even a government building) directly connected with your child's preadoptive life. Take lots of pictures so your child will have a record of the experience.

Ask foreign students or other natives of your child's country for names of relatives who might have children about the same age as your child. Encourage your child and one of these children to become pen pals. Try to arrange a meeting of the pen pals as a highlight of the trip. This will help your child understand daily life in her native country and reduce her discomfort with some of what she sees (i.e., poverty, beggars, people living in huts or on the street).

Help your child understand that people can be happy even if they don't have the material things Americans often believe they need. Try to find a friend or an institution (such as a school or your child's orphanage), which she, your family, or possibly her class, can "adopt" and continue to help when she returns home. Your child is likely to be less upset about some of what she has seen if she feels that she is doing something to help. Such projects also are always excellent for building self-esteem and family unity.

CHAPTER 15

# Special Needs Adoptions

Throughout the world, "special children" are waiting for adoption. Some are blind or deaf. Others have been crippled by polio. Some have genetic defects such as cleft palates or heart problems that can be surgically corrected in the United States, but not in their home countries. Still others are healthy, but they're older or they belong to sibling groups. All need parents, homes, and love.

It takes a special gift to parent one of these children. Increasingly, foreign adoption agencies are actively recruiting parents with the strength and experience to raise such children. In this chapter we will discuss:

- Requirements for parenting children with special needs
- Services available to parents
- Adopting sibling groups

## REQUIREMENTS FOR PARENTING SPECIAL NEEDS CHILDREN

When Joan gets a call about a child overseas with medical problems, she starts hunting for parents with the qualifications to raise him. Social workers call this process "specificity." There are no waiting lists for such placements. Social workers turn to veteran adoptive families they know or to applicants with experience in working with children with handicapping conditions.

Research shows that excellent parents for children with special needs tend to fit one of these profiles:

- They are mature couples (usually in their mid-thirties to mid-forties) with more than two children. They have extremely strong marriages. The mothers have made a career of motherhood. They either know how to find the services children with special needs require or are willing to learn. Usually they are of middle income. The poor don't have the resources that kids with special needs require, and upper-income families often aren't willing to commit the time. They're too busy with their careers.
- They are single parents with backgrounds in health, education, or social service. They have worked with children who have medical or other problems, and they know how to cope with such difficulties. They have good insurance and flexible schedules.

Successful parents of children with special needs share certain other characteristics:

- They have a highly realistic notion of what children are like.
- They work to help a child develop his or her potential, but their egos do not depend on the success of perfect children.
- They are flexible.
- They have a great deal of love to give, but understand that they must meet their own needs in order to meet the needs of their children.

Some people prefer the term "challenged" children to children with special needs. It's a more positive way of looking at the situation. Whatever the terminology, these children require "challenged" parents.

What should you do if special needs adoption interests you? Call an adoption agency, but be prepared for a letdown. Often a social worker will greet a request to adopt a child with special needs with caution or suspicion if she doesn't know you. This may hurt your feelings since you want to do something important and difficult. However, there are reasons for the social worker's reserve.

She's looking for experience in working with children with handicaps. She'll ask you if you've ever been around such children, either because you're related to one or have worked with children with handicapping conditions. She must be sure that you are capable of coping with your child's problems. You adopt such a child for life and it takes enormous long-term patience and energy to cope. This isn't a six-month project or one you can give up when the going gets rough. A child's life is at stake. If you've never adopted or worked with children with problems, your worker is well advised to be cautious.

If you have a strong feeling that this is something you can and should do, demonstrate your commitment by asking what training you need to qualify. This will impress your worker. She may suggest programs in which you could enroll or volunteer work you could do to prepare for such an adoption. If you follow through, you probably will end up on her list of parents to call when the need arises.

Many parents of "challenged" foreign-born children initially adopted healthy international children. They gradually became more involved in foreign adoption or met other adoptive families of children with special needs, became interested in doing something similar and were recruited by a social worker.

## SERVICES FOR ADOPTED CHILDREN WITH SPECIAL NEEDS

You must meet U.S. Immigration and Naturalization Service income requirements to adopt a foreign child with special needs. This means you must have too much money to qualify for welfare medical assistance. However, there are other services and programs that can help you meet the challenges of adopting a foreign child with special needs. Consider the following ideas for meeting medical, educational, home modification, and socialization needs.

### Medical

- Check your family health coverage. Does it cover pre-existing conditions? If so, your child will qualify for all benefits.

Many parents of children with special needs work for employers who provide very good medical insurance.

- Contact a private hospital or health clinic to see if it will provide free or reduced price services. If you have religious ties with such institutions, seek assistance from your clergyperson.
- Check your state's services for children with handicapping conditions. Names vary from state to state. Your state welfare or social-services department or local United Way can refer you to the proper office. You may qualify for free equipment such as wheelchairs, braces, and the like. You may also qualify for free procedures. Such programs have enabled many families to adopt children with special needs.
- Check with various health agencies such as Shriners, Easter Seals, or the March of Dimes. Do they have services that could benefit your child? Your public library will have books listing local and national service-providing agencies.

## Education

Public school districts are required to provide equal education for all children, including those with handicapping conditions. This might mean that services could begin in the preschool years.

- Contact your local public school district or school principal for information about its special education program.
- When your child arrives, have the school district do a social-psychological and medical evaluation. This is the critical step. Your child will receive only those services indicated on the evaluation. If you are not satisfied with the evaluation, you may ask for further testing by an independent testing agency. Each state has an office where a child's individual educational plan can be discussed.
- Be sure that the school district personnel are sensitive to the communications and cultural difficulties of assessing a foreign child. Some children of normal intelligence have been mistakenly labeled as mentally handicapped when their difficulty is with learning academic English (a process that can take several years).
- You can have your child assessed at other agencies, including local university testing centers, private schools that specialize

in various handicaps, private clinics, and private mental health organizations. Such assessments may help you get the services you need from the school district.

- If you can afford it, you might consider placing your child in a private educational program for persons with handicaps. Your child might receive enough specialized assistance in a relatively short time to go into regular public school classes.

## Socialization

Your child will need more than medical and educational services to grow into a happy, healthy adult. Consider the following ideas:

- Is there a parent self-help group for your child's handicap? You can meet families coping with the same difficulties, and your child can make friends with other children who are similarly "challenged." You can find such groups by calling United Way or the public library or checking the Yellow Pages. Other parents often are your best source of referrals to services.
- Do you have a youth agency, such as a Boys and Girls Club or Girls, Inc., which welcomes children with handicaps? This may be a great way for your child to participate in activities with a wide range of children.
- Does your church include children with handicaps in its youth programs? If not, try to find a church that does. Check the Yellow Pages for listings of churches and other buildings that are accessible to people with handicapping conditions.
- Is there a Scout troop that your child could join? Is there a Little League for children with special needs? What about Special Olympics? These can help your child experience the rewards of participating, competing, and achieving.

## Home Modifications

Your home may need modifications to accommodate a child with a handicapping condition. If you aren't a do-it-yourselfer and funds are scarce, look for creative ways of getting such work done at a cost you can afford.

136

- Call a community college, vocational school, or high school shop teacher. Would a class like to work on your home as a project?
- Does the instructor know of any retired craftsmen who might be willing to help you for a modest fee? Some excellent amateur workmen take up such projects in retirement and might enjoy the experience.
- Place an item inquiring about such help in your church bulletin or neighborhood newsletter.

Craftspersons may come up with ingenious solutions to problems. For example, Eileen's grandfather built an "elevator" that took his wife upstairs for the last twenty years of her life. The "elevator" consisted of a wooden box raised and lowered by an electronic pulley. You may be astonished at what can be done.

## ADOPTING SIBLING GROUPS

Some prospective parents inquire about adopting sibling groups, thinking that it might be easier to go through the adoption process once instead of twice. Usually Joan discourages such ideas unless the parents are very mature and experienced. Normally, the adoption of siblings is the most difficult challenge a parent can undertake.

Most such groups consist of two to six children of varying ages, of whom at least one or two are older. You may even be dealing with teenagers. These children have a strong sense of an existing family unit in which the oldest child has already assumed the parental role. The others tend to play varying roles such as baby or middle child.

In such families, the oldest makes the decisions and the younger ones look to the oldest for guidance. The oldest child is extremely reluctant to relinquish this role, and the younger children will continue to look to the oldest—not the adoptive parents—for authority.

These children have survived by strongly bonding with one another and treating outsiders with suspicion. The adoptive parents will be outsiders for a very long time—maybe always. The children will support one another in any battles with the adoptive parents and will protect any individual child who is in conflict with the adoptive parents. Under such circumstances, a game is constantly played called "odd man out." The odd man out is invariably the adoptive parent.

Of all special needs children, Joan considers sibling groups the neediest. Parents capable of meeting such challenges generally are:

- Mature couples with a great deal of parenting experience and extremely strong marriages. They have strong individual self-concepts and form a united front in dealing with the children.
- Couples who are willing to give a tremendous amount of love, with no expectation of receiving love or gratitude soon or ever.
- Couples who understand that at least once a week, they must get away from the children to renew their personal resources. If they don't "fill their buckets," there will be nothing left to give during the following week.
- Couples who are good at giving children positive reinforcement.
- Couples who can love a child and dislike her behavior. They manage to simultaneously communicate their love while working to correct the behavior—a real art.

Even experienced couples who adopt sibling groups must be willing to accept family counseling or therapy. They may find that they are dealing with problems they can't solve.

Adoptive parents who successfully raise sibling groups have the satisfaction of knowing they have met the most difficult adoption challenge. In many cases, their efforts prevent such children from being "lost" as human beings. That's a pretty remarkable accomplishment.

## SUMMARY

It takes a special gift to adopt a child with special needs or a sibling group. Except in unusual circumstances, it is probably not a good option for parents adopting for the first time or who have never had biological children or worked extensively with children. Such parents probably will find themselves fully challenged by a child without a handicapping condition. However, if you are attracted to such a possibility, don't give up the idea. Gain some experience in parenting. Start volunteering with children with handicapping conditions. Take a class that would prepare you to work with a particular special need (sign language, for example). Then talk to your social worker. As with everything else in adoption, if your heart is telling you loudly to do something, there's probably a reason.

# CHAPTER 16

# Joan's Story

## Mindy

It was a rainy morning, the type of morning when it always happened. My Korean daughter, Mindy, stopped me.

"Um. Mommy."

"Yes, Mindy."

"You know, um, day like today. You know, um, day like today." (During her recitation of this now familiar litany, she always repeated everything.)

"You mean a rainy day?"

"Yes, Mommy. My grandma, she borrow a car. We go a long way, Mommy. We go up a hill and down a hill. My grandma, she borrow a car. We go a long way, Mommy. We go up a hill, down a hill. Then, Mommy, my grandma say we lost. We get out. She say, 'You sit here on this bench and I go buy you candy.' I say, 'Grandma, I not move.' I wait a long time, Mommy, but my grandma, she not come back. My grandma, she not know where I am, Mommy. My grandma, she worry about me."

It was Mindy's only memory of Korea. Days like this always brought it back. Even though her grandma had abandoned her, Mindy still loved her and was concerned that her grandma was worried about her and "missing her."

"Mindy," I said. "Let's write your grandma a letter. Then she'll know where you are and she won't worry." From then on, the recitations grew less frequent, but they were burned into my memory along with everything else surrounding the adoption of my lovely daughter.

Our road to adoption started with a news program I happened to watch in 1973. Before that newscast from Vietnam changed our lives, we were a pretty typical middle American family. My husband, Ray, and I had met as teenagers growing up in Omaha in the 1950s, then fell in love several years after we graduated. Ray had served in Korea at the end of the war and never forgot the children he saw there.

He always said that we should adopt, but the possibility was remote. A year after we were married in 1957, our son Randy was born. Two years later, Bob came along, followed by Raelynn ten months later. I stopped working to care for the children. We could survive on Ray's postal-worker salary, but there wasn't much spare cash.

One morning in the early 1970s, after I had taken Ray to work and the children to school, I happened to catch a TV news special about orphans in Vietnam. The piece featured a little girl who was tied to a tree because she always ran away. In that moment, my whole life changed. I cried into my coffee cup and could not stop for hours. I remembered what Ray had said about adoption.

"Did you mean it when you said we might adopt?" I asked when he came home that night.

"Yes," he replied.

Neither of us knew where to call or how to go about adopting an Oriental child, but we knew we had to do it. I just knew that somewhere there was a child who needed us.

I started calling the adoption agencies listed in the Yellow Pages and got the distinct message "don't call us, we'll call you." None of them knew or cared anything about foreign adoption. A representative of the county social-services department told me flatly that foreign adoption was impossible. But I wouldn't give up.

I told my mother-in-law what we were thinking about, not sure of her reaction. To my delight, she mentioned that she had met an American woman with several Oriental children at a garage sale at the woman's home. She described the house and its general location. She remembered that there had been a trunk on the front porch. That was all.

141

I set out to find the woman. If she had managed to adopt, so could we. It was January 2 and Omaha was having a mini-blizzard. I drove over icy hills to the area and started looking for the house. The winds howled and the snow blew.

After four or five blocks, I spotted a green house with a trunk still on the porch. Could this be the house? Now that I was here, what did I do? I whispered a little prayer. My stomach was in knots. This was terribly difficult for me, but as I turned briefly to retreat to my car, I remembered the little girl who haunted me. I knocked on the door.

A four-year-old girl with big, bright, almond-shaped eyes answered. She looked just like the little girl from Vietnam! I was on the right track. She was followed by her American mother who was on the phone. I told her who I was and said I wanted to adopt.

"Do you have a home study?" she asked.

"Where do I get a home study?" I asked.

"Call this lady in Lincoln. I can't talk to you now. Call me back in a week. Here's my phone number." She handed me her number and the number in Lincoln. Then she shut the door and went on with her phone conversation.

The follow-up phone calls were difficult. The woman at the state department of social services in Lincoln said I could only get a home study if an agency requested one. The woman with the children was abrupt. She gave us the name of a possible adoption contact or two and let it go at that.

Ray and I told our other children what we were thinking about. The adoption then became a family pursuit. We decided we wanted a girl because we had only one girl.

We wrote to agencies, asking for a child from birth through age four. I especially wanted a toddler since I knew I was good at working with children that age. Finally we heard from one of the agencies that we would have to wait at least a year and a half for a child that young but we could have a child aged four to seven after a home study was completed.

We really wanted a younger child. What should we do? We waited as long as we could to answer, prayed about our decision, then said we would take an older child. If the child was seven, so what? But in my heart of hearts, I wanted a child who was five or younger.

Meanwhile we had to get a home study done. Now that I have done hundreds of home studies for other people, I laugh at the way I prepared. I cleaned the entire house—including moving and cleaning behind the refrigerator. I cleaned so vigorously that I threw my back out. And again I wondered if we would be approved. I worried that we didn't have enough bedrooms, enough money and enough of this and enough of that. The social worker came and stayed three and a half hours! Then she made two more visits that long.

Finally on the last visit, my husband asked if we had been approved. She said she saw no problems. She said she thought we could provide a wonderful home for a child from overseas. Imagine my joy! Our child—the child meant for us—would come!

We waited for a referral from either Korea or Vietnam. When we got the call from our local social worker that we had a daughter, Mindy's pictures were a shock. She was supposed to be seven, but she looked no more than five. She had a crew cut, wore slacks and a shirt, and had a frown that made her look like she was about to cry. She looked like a boy.

"I thought we were getting a girl," I told the worker.

"You are," she replied.

Mindy's story was sad. She had been abandoned on a street corner. After she was found, she was taken to a hospital because she had ringworm over her entire body. As I looked at the pathetic picture and heard the story, somewhere from deep inside a voice said that this is a child who needs *you*. By 4:30 P.M. that day, we had filed all the papers needed to bring her to the United States.

Then the hardest part of our adoption process began. For three months, we waited for our daughter to come. Every day was agony. I worried about her health. Who was taking care of her? Was she okay? For weeks, I waited by the telephone, thinking that a call would come about her arrival. Ray and I took turns doing necessary errands. I think now how much easier it would have been if there had been telephone answering machines in those days!

When *the* call finally came in late September 1974, Ray was on "phone duty" and took down the information with what he had at hand—an eyebrow pencil. "Arrive 9/27 - KCM, 730-P - Worker Name?? Forgot??" the scribbled message read.

We flew to Kansas City to get Mindy. Although her plane wasn't due until 7:30 P.M., we were off by 6:00 A.M. We waited twelve hours at the airport. When the flight finally arrived late, they had to summon us by loudspeaker.

Mindy and a group of babies came off the plane after the other passengers. I was shocked. She was beautiful! Her hair had grown and she was tiny—maybe a size three.

"My daughter," I thought. "My daughter is finally in my arms."

I got my first inkling of what life with Mindy would be like when I took her to the bathroom. I put her in a stall and used another. When I came out, Mindy was gone. I panicked. Then she jumped out from behind a big trash can and said "boo Umma!" We were in for the time of our lives.

Mindy, who turned out to be five, was terrified and very withdrawn at first. She spent most of her time sitting on the couch and working puzzles. We think she had been abused, but she has blocked out most memories of her early childhood. We communicated mainly in sign language.

After about two weeks, she began to explore the house. When I heard her opening and closing cupboard doors, I knew she was beginning to lose her fear. However, I sensed that she was still grieving for what she had left behind and my heart ached for her. But I didn't know what to do or say to make it better for her.

One day, she began crying. Although she still didn't speak much English and I spoke no Korean, I could feel she was crying for the mother she had left in Korea and would never see again. I wanted so badly to be the mother she needed, but I didn't know what to do. I could feel her hurt. I hurt because she hurt. So I did all that I could do. I picked her up and held her tight.

"Honey, we're in this thing together," I told her. "I'll never leave you. You go ahead and cry and I'll cry with you." She cried and cried—and so did I. We had reached the turning point. After that, she was home. She was ours.

I will never forget that day—the day Mindy really became my daughter. It taught me something terribly important about foreign adoption. No matter how much the children gain, they also have lost whatever went before. They need time to adjust and time to grieve. Sometimes new adoptive parents are hurt by this. They don't understand. They may inadvertently deny their children the necessary time and space to grieve.

This is a serious mistake, especially with a somewhat older child like Mindy. Foreign adopted children, even babies, know that they have experienced a major change. They need permission to feel what they are feeling. In time, with love and patience, they will fully accept their new lives and new families. But they need to sense, as Mindy apparently did, that their new Moms and Dads understand what they're going through.

With the big barrier overcome, Mindy rapidly became a real part of our family. She learned English, partially with the aid of television, which she enjoyed watching. We realized how much she had learned and could understand one day when Raelynn decided to take her roller skating and tried to explain this to her in a combination of sign language and simple sentences. Mindy shrugged, continued watching television and ignored Raelynn.

"Mom, what shall I do? My ride is about to come and I can't get Mindy to understand," Raelynn asked me in desperation.

"Oh, just let her keep watching cartoons. There'll be other days when you can take her skating," I said.

Then we heard footsteps coming down the stairs. A minute later Mindy appeared, dressed to go roller skating and holding Raelynn's roller skates.

"Let's go," Mindy said.

There were other signs of growing acceptance. When Mindy first started going to school, she drew houses with Korean roofs and mothers with long black hair. Eventually the pictures changed to gable roofs and mothers with curly blond hair like mine. Mindy's life was not the only one changed by her adoption. My future changed profoundly.

## MY CAREER

Before Mindy's adoption, the idea of a career in social work had never occurred to me. Because of what I experienced in attempting to do a foreign adoption in a city with no agency, I realized there was a need to provide such a service locally.

I decided to make foreign adoption my career. I returned to college and acquired bachelor's and master's degrees in social work from the University of Nebraska at Omaha. In 1981, Holt International Children's Services opened a Nebraska office and I became its first staff member. In 1986, I opened Kids Each Served in Love (KESIL), a small adoption agency.

Today I'm a Certified Master of Social Work specializing in international adoption. My agency, KESIL, places children from Thailand, Honduras, Guatemala, Eastern Europe, El Salvador, Peru, Korea, Nicaragua, and the United States.

However, I have often thought that my experience as an adoptive mother is as important to my work as my professional credentials. When I meet someone who desperately wants a child, I remember how much I wanted Mindy and our second Korean daughter, Jodi. When I walk into someone's house for a home study, I remember how terrified I felt the first time the social worker entered my home. When I give parents a picture of their child, I remember our joy when we received our pictures of Mindy and Jodi.

This understanding of what it means to go through the adoption process has kept me in the field all these years. Every child I place is a victory for children who need parents.

As for Mindy today, life is good. She is working her way through college, sharing an apartment with Jodi. This is something of a minor miracle, since Mindy is reserved and very precise about her housekeeping and Jodi is just the opposite. Mindy is still beautiful. Heads turn when she walks down the street.

She has come to terms with her past. She visited Korea once, but did it strictly American-style. She stayed in a Western-style hostel. She didn't want to go to the orphanage or hospital where she had stayed. She had no desire to try to find anyone who had known her. Unlike Jodi she cannot imagine wanting to reunite with her birth family. She says her American family *is* her family. Period.

We remain extremely proud of both daughters and respect their different attitudes towards dealing with their origins and their adoptions. Both have enriched and blessed our lives beyond measure.

## Jodi

"If you don't call me in three hours, I'm calling the Korean police."

I stood holding onto the door of my Seoul hotel room, in agony, as my adopted twenty-two-year-old daughter Jodi left with the Korean mother, brothers, and sister with whom she had just been reunited.

For beautiful, strong-willed Jodi, the reunion was a dream come true. Ever since being placed for adoption at age eight, she had prayed she would find her birth family. She deeply loved me and other members of our family, but she had never forgotten her Korean mother and an older brother to whom she was especially close.

The longing to see them again never left her. I knew this. I knew Jodi would never be completely happy until she found her original family. That was why I had always kept information in Jodi's Korean file indicating that she would welcome contact with the birth family.

When the astonishing message from the Korean agency had arrived three months earlier, I had been almost as thrilled as Jodi. But now that the reunion had begun, I realized how threatened and unprepared I was. What if I never saw Jodi again? What if Jodi chose to stay in Korea? What if Jodi's Korean family kidnapped her? I wouldn't even know how to call them. There was nothing to do but wait. It was a nightmare.

I remember feeling every kind of emotion you could possibly feel. I cried. I paced. I couldn't sleep. I stared at the phone, waiting for the three hours to be up. Ray called, wanting to know how the reunion went. I lied and told him "fine." Finally Jodi called. Immediately after I knew she was okay, I felt guilty.

Why shouldn't she be okay? She was with her family. And besides, Jodi isn't a baby. She's a college student who lives in her own apartment. She has her own life. I don't interfere with it.

But this was different. I felt very alone and very threatened. For the next few days, Jodi stayed with her Korean family, but called me every day. I often saw her during the day. I think she had begun to realize how hard this was for me. Gradually I began to feel less an outsider, especially with Jodi's Korean mother.

I liked her a great deal. Despite our difficulties in communicating, I came to realize that she is a very courageous woman—spunky, like Jodi. I got new insights into Jodi. I came away with deeper appreciation and respect. I began to realize that Jodi was still my daughter, as she also would always be her Korean mother's daughter. She would love us both, but in different ways. This realization was critical. It helped me cope with the trauma of the reunion and strengthened my relationship with my daughter.

During the reunion, I kept remembering the separate tragedies that had led to our becoming mother and daughter. From these tragedies, we had built something good and beautiful. Jodi's reunion with her Korean family could not weaken those bonds.

After adopting Mindy, Ray and I wanted to adopt another Korean child. We saw Jodi's picture in *Maryknoll Magazine*. We had fallen in love with her. We contacted a friend who gave us the phone number of the priest who ran the orphanage where Jodi was living. However, soon after we contacted the orphanage, Ray was seriously injured. He was out of work for months. Our income was reduced to his disability pay. Meanwhile, a series of heavy expenses hit us. A water main had broken, running up an enormous bill. The city was demanding the removal of six dis-eased elm trees. The kitchen stove wasn't working.

One hot, humid, late summer day, I sent the children off with their friends so I could try to think of a way to adopt Jodi. I went over and over the situation. As much as we wanted her, we just couldn't afford adoption costs and transportation expenses on top of all our bills. I would have to call the orphanage and free Jodi for adoption by another family. I was devastated, but could see no alternative.

I went to the phone and tried to call Korea. The line was busy. Then I got busy with other things. Later I spent a quiet evening with Ray, watching television.

Late that evening we were sitting in our bedroom when the phone rang. Ray's mother shouted, "Come quick. Grandma's been stabbed."

An intruder had persuaded Ray's eighty-three-year-old grand-mother to allow him to use her phone. He tried to rob her. When she resisted, he stabbed her twenty-two times. When we arrived at Grandma's house, she was still conscious but terribly wounded. The police were there.

Grandma was taken to a hospital for surgery, but it was hope-less. For two days, she suffered terribly, then she died. For a time, we were so preoccupied with this tragedy that we put all thoughts of adoption on hold.

One day, just when I had decided to call the orphanage to say we could not adopt Jodi, Ray's mother called—this time with happy news. Ray was the beneficiary of an insurance policy Grandma had recently taken out. The policy provided the amount we needed to adopt Jodi—to the penny.

So finally I called the orphanage to say we could hardly wait to adopt Jodi. We had our home study updated and completed our forms. Then we waited impatiently for our daughter. If I had known how Jodi was suffering at the time, the wait would have been even harder.

Jodi, of course, knew nothing of this. She was struggling to survive her own catastrophe. Jodi was born in 1968 on Chindo Island, the youngest of four children. Her father deserted the family after his business failed in the economic depression that hit Korea in the 1970s.

Jodi moved to Seoul and was cared for by her older sister and brother while her mother worked as a housemaid. She saw her mother only on weekends. During one visit, her mother asked if she would like to go to America. This sounded fine to eight-year-old Jodi until her fifteen-year-old brother warned her that she would have to go by herself. She cried and begged her mother not to send her away.

But her mother felt that the best thing she could do for Jodi was to place her for adoption since the family could not support her until she would be old enough to work. Then Jodi begged for the family address so she would know where to find them. Her older sister failed to give it to her. Jodi was turned over to an orphanage and began the worst nine or ten months of her life. She missed her family terribly. She ran away frequently.

She isolated herself from everyone at the orphanage and begged God to save her. Later she told us that when she learned she had a new family waiting in America, she could hardly wait to leave. When her plane landed in Omaha, she ran to us, hugged us, and talked a mile a minute. This was in great contrast to Mindy's initial reserve. Would this adoption be easier?

To me the day was especially significant. It was one year to the day after Ray's grandmother had died. Jodi's new middle name was "Ellen" in honor of her late great-grandmother, who had given her "a legacy of life."

149

Jodi's spunk resembled Grandma's. She needed all her pluck to cope with the adjustment to her new life. Although she was almost nine, we had been told that she was six. We treated her accordingly. We put her in school with children three years younger, not realizing the effect this would have. She was more mature than her classmates and could not relate to them. They made fun of her. She spent many hours crying. As a result, she missed Korea even more.

In spite of her problems, she loved us and became very close to our family, especially to Mindy. But she did not forget her Korean family. As soon as Jodi could speak English, she talked about her mother, her sister, and her two brothers. She insisted "I am not an orphan."

I noticed the pronounced differences between Mindy and Jodi. Mindy came with a lot of issues resolved and very few memories. Jodi arrived with lots of memories and very few issues resolved. She always felt rejected because her family gave her up. Because of these feelings, Jodi always felt she had something to prove. She became very competitive.

The issue of Jodi's birth family never left us. We stayed in touch with the orphanage in Korea. We placed a letter in her adoption file stating that we were willing to be contacted by the birth family. Every time I went to Korea on adoption business, I checked for news of Jodi's family.

In 1989, I took Jodi to Korea and we left one last letter in the file. We agreed that if this letter did not produce results, we would make no further attempts to contact her family. Jodi agreed that she could come to terms with the possibility of never again seeing her birth family.

However, this time it worked. In November of 1990, Jodi's older sister visited the agency that had handled the adoption and asked for additional information on her sister. She did so because she felt guilty over not giving Jodi the family's address. Besides, their mother was aging and grieving for Jodi.

The agency wrote to me with information about the family and "respectfully requested" updated information. When I received the letter, I called Jodi and asked if I could drop over. Jodi said sure, but she was very curious about what was going on. We both have extremely busy schedules and I don't normally stop by just to chat. When I arrived, she took one look at me and said, "Mother, what's wrong?"

"What's the one thing in all your life that you've ever wanted if you could have only one wish?" I asked.

"My family," she breathed, so softly I could hardly hear.

"Merry Christmas, Happy Easter, Happy Birthday, happy every day of your life!" I said, handing her the letter. As she read, all she could say over and over was, "Oh, my gosh! Oh, my gosh!"

The letter told Jodi her life story. It confirmed what she had told us all along. She was not an orphan. She had a mother, two brothers, and a sister. Her recollections of those early years were accurate.

As soon as she recovered from the shock, Jodi said, "I have to see them."

"That's all been arranged," I said. "We'll go after Christmas."

Jodi and I would escort children being adopted by Americans. Soon after, the enormity of what was happening began to hit Jodi. I tried to help her cope with her feelings, which seemed to be a mixture of love, desire to see them again, and anger over having been placed for adoption.

She talked about her memories of the orphanage and seemed angry at her Korean mother. I told Jodi that had her Korean mother known what would happen, she wouldn't have placed her for adoption. I tried to comfort her by saying that I was sure her Korean mother had thought she was making Jodi's life better.

I also told Jodi that it was okay for her to resent her Korean mother because she had unintentionally caused her great pain. At the time, Jodi thought she would share her feelings with her Korean mother, but later decided not to. Perhaps it would be better for her Korean mother to see her happy.

It was a scared but happy Jodi who went to Korea. She found that her relatives were prospering in various businesses and that they all had personalities similar to hers. She became instantly close to her favorite brother. They made plans for him to visit her in the United States. I thought Jodi especially resembled her older sister.

By the time we left Seoul, I felt quite close to her family. The resemblances were very important to Jodi. She told me that for the first time since leaving Korea, she felt that she really fit somewhere.

A few people in our family had been concerned that Jodi might not return to the United States. But she did come home. She always knew she would. She plans to go to Korea at least yearly, but will remain an American. She says she doesn't want her relationship with us to change.

Adoption permanently altered the course of Jodi's life. She will always be Korean and she will always be American. She will always love and be loved by two families. She says now that she's glad she was adopted and that we adopted her. Now Jodi is more comfortable with who she is and how she became that way. We all have noticed a remarkable change in her since the reunion. She is much more self-assured and more trusting of other people. Finding her family has changed the way she relates to other people and analyzes situations.

As for me, Jodi's mother, I would do it all again. I would adopt her. I would love her unconditionally, and I would let her go again. The reunion has taught me that expanding our family circle has simply increased the amount of love we experience.

We said in the introduction that often you see resemblances between your adopted children and other members of your family. When I look at Jodi—so bright, beautiful, and courageous—I see a reflection of the great-grandmother she never knew. I know that Grandma is terribly proud of her namesake and grateful that such great good came from her personal catastrophe.

# CHAPTER 17

# Eileen's Story

## Raj

It was just after midnight, September 25, 1981. The Omaha airport was nearly deserted. An iron grate blocked access to the gates. We paced, waiting for the late flight from St. Louis.

Our son was aboard that plane—the last leg of his trip from Mother Teresa's orphanage in New Delhi to his new home here. What a long, hard road had brought us to this time and place!

My husband, Ron Psota, and I were sixties kids from large Nebraska Catholic farm families. We had met at the University of Nebraska, but parted for two years while Ron served in the Peace Corps in southern India. We had kept in close touch by mail the entire time and got engaged several months after he returned home.

Ron had come back to the United States in love with India and other Asian countries and cultures. I knew that India would be part of the rest of our lives.

Our lives were busy. I was a newspaper reporter and Ron a city planner. We both volunteered for everything in sight. Friends were drawn by Ron's warm hospitality and spectacular Indian cooking. When Vietnam fell in 1975, one of his Peace Corps friends talked us into sponsoring a family of Cambodian refugees. Later we were involved with Laotian, Vietnamese, Afghan, and Polish refugees. We also became a host family for the first of numerous foreign students.

For years we never considered having children. Very few of our friends did. Children weren't "in" during the early seventies. Besides, we were too busy. Between our paid and volunteer jobs, we were putting in about sixty-five or seventy hours a week. But as I drew nearer my thirtieth birthday, the lack of children began to depress me. On a Christmas trip to India in 1976, it hit hard. What was I doing in India? Why wasn't I home baking, cooking, and hanging stockings? I wanted a child.

Ron seemed happy with our life as it was. He was the most doting uncle in both families and a surrogate father to a dozen young Laotian refugees who had arrived without parents. I loved the refugee kids, but I wanted a more permanent relationship.

I stopped taking the pill. Nothing happened. My doctor discovered a fertility problem, which medication might correct but I was frightened of possible long-term effects. A sixth sense told me that we probably were not meant to become biological parents.

I wanted to adopt, but I decided not to discuss it with Ron until I had gathered information about foreign adoption. I wasn't sure I could persuade him to adopt, but if I did, I knew it would be a foreign child, preferably Indian. I couldn't imagine people whose lives were as international as ours competing for the limited supply of white children.

As a reporter covering social-service agencies, I had easy access to information about adoption. I knew social workers involved in adoption. I also knew a family that had adopted several Korean children. Still, the calls for appointments were among the most difficult of my life. It was terribly hard to admit that I had a problem and needed help. It was especially difficult to accept the power that agencies now had over our future. It made us so terribly vulnerable—an uncomfortable position for anyone, but even more difficult for a reporter who was used to being in control. Fortunately my friend with the four Korean kids was extremely encouraging.

"I talk to a lot of people about adoption," she said over lunch. "I think you're actually going to do this."

My research with agencies confirmed what I had suspected: domestic agency adoptions were extremely difficult except for children with special needs. It might be possible to adopt a biracial child, but many social workers discouraged this. None of the local agencies I talked to knew much about foreign adoption. Holt International Children's Services had an office in Omaha, but I didn't even call because years earlier I had received information that said mothers were required to stop working for at least eighteen months. That was impossible.

One night in the car, I finally talked to Ron about adoption. I had my speech all prepared, but I had underestimated his ability to read my mind.

"Would you mind terribly if we considered adoption? I think—"

He stopped me in mid-sentence. "I'm surprised it's taken you this long to bring it up," he said. "I've been expecting you to want to adopt for a long time."

"Then it's okay with you?" I asked, too happy to almost believe what I was hearing. "We could get a little girl from India."

It was that simple. We both pictured the same thing—a beautiful little girl from India whom we would name Shanti (Peace), the word we had inscribed on our wedding rings. We assumed we would adopt a girl because very few boys are available from India due to the higher value Indians place on males.

We weren't sure how we were going to get her since none of the agencies I had talked to were involved in foreign adoption. However, no reporter/former Peace Corps volunteer couple would be deterred by a minor detail like this! We knew that children had been adopted from India and assumed that eventually we would figure out a way to do it.

We wrote to orphanages and lawyers that Ron knew in India. Over the next four or five months, the discouraging responses came back. None of the people or organizations we contacted were involved in foreign adoption. Nor did they suggest alternatives. We wouldn't give up. There had to be a way to adopt an Indian child. Somehow we would find it.

We told no one what we were planning. We knew our relatives and friends would be extremely enthusiastic—and drive us crazy with questions. We wanted to wait until we had specific information about an adoption agency working in India that might accept us. By accident, my sister in St. Louis supplied the key.

"I've got some friends here who have just adopted a little girl from India," said Pat casually one night during a routine phone call.

My heart beat faster. "Could you give their names? There's something important we haven't told you. We want to adopt from India. Maybe they could tell us how to do it."

"They went through Mother Teresa," Pat said. "You can call them and find out who they worked with in the United States."

Trembling, I made a quick call to the number in St. Louis that Pat had given me. The couple referred us to Kathy Sreedhar of Washington, D.C., Mother Teresa's volunteer American representative. Kathy told us to get a home study done, and then she would send us information. We were launched!

The home study was no fun. We chose a local agency with which we had worked closely for five years on refugee resettlement. We thought our close ties would simplify the approval process even though adoption was a different program. We were wrong.

The social worker was pleasant, but acted as if the agency had never heard of us. We spent hours answering questions about our backgrounds and our ability to relate to a child who was "different." We found the process almost demeaning in light of our experience in working with international people. We sensed that our caseworker rather enjoyed the power she had over us. But we knew we had to jump through her hoops to win the agency's approval.

The first letter we received from Kathy Sreedhar would have discouraged all but the most determined:

> The children suffer from a variety of diseases, come from unknown backgrounds, and there is no guarantee how they will develop or behave. Little if anything is known about the child's biological family. . . . The children usually suffer from one or more of the following: malnourishment, vitamin and protein deficiency, diarrhea and intestinal parasites and worms, skin diseases (e.g., lice, scabies, boils), upper respiratory and ear infections, rickets, poor teeth, enlarged liver, malaria, and positive tuberculosis.

It continued in this vein for several more paragraphs. It forced me to face what a foreign adoption might entail. I knew from my research that there were indeed risks of health problems and learning disabilities. Of course it was important to warn people about what might happen. But then I asked myself an important question: What could they tell us about India that Ron hadn't seen?

I proceeded with our application, knowing that adopting through Mother Teresa was the closest thing to a pure act of faith that I would ever make. It made me all the more grateful when our child turned out to be beautiful, bright, and abnormally healthy.

The application repeated many of the questions we had already answered for our home study. It asked for specifics as to why we wanted to adopt from India. I assumed Ron's Peace Corps service and our half-Indian life-style would be strong points in our favor. But what did you say if you simply wanted to do this?

In August 1980, Kathy called and said we had been approved. We would be at the top of the waiting list for the next group of children. She would contact us between January and April with news of a specific child.

It seemed almost too easy. The months flew by. I changed careers—from reporting to corporate public relations. The new job paid better and had more regular hours. It would work much better for a baby. This was the best of all worlds!

Beginning in January, I started waiting for the phone to ring. When no call came in January or February, I wasn't worried. However by mid-April, I was concerned. On a business trip to Washington, D.C., I called Kathy to see if we would have news soon.

"Why didn't you answer my letter?" she asked.

"What letter?" I replied, feeling sick in the stomach.

"The one I sent asking for more information. Since you didn't answer, we assumed you weren't interested."

Before I could blurt out more frantic questions, Kathy told me she was in the midst of a family crisis and couldn't talk. She said to call back in three hours. I knew that she was doing all this as a volunteer, and it placed a tremendous burden on her and her family. Like all adoptive parents, I was enormously grateful to her for this incredibly unselfish service. But at the moment all I could think of was whether we would get a child. I sat staring dumbly at the hotel room walls. Three eternal hours.

What could have gone wrong? What letter was she talking about? Why hadn't she called us? What could we do now? Would we ever get a child? Had only five minutes passed?

When 10:00 P.M. finally arrived, Kathy was still unable to tell me anything, but she said she would try to find out what was happening and let me know.

"Maybe it would help if you met me," I said. "I have to come to Washington again next week. Could you possibly see me then?"

Kathy asked me to have dinner at her home the following Wednesday. But I was scared and discouraged—probably unnecessarily so.

The next day, a Friday, was the longest of my life. Early that morning, I called my cousin, Marylou, in Nebraska, weeping as we talked. Marylou was unruffled.

"If this were a magazine subscription, they would have written at least three times," she said.

I flew home and told Ron what little I knew. It was hard to be cheerful, but there was no sense in giving up. If something had gone wrong, it could surely be fixed. If people with our credentials, connections, and determination couldn't adopt, who could?

The experience had overtones of the years I had waited for Ron to come back from India. I had survived the loneliness of those years with the help of two songs: Peter, Paul & Mary's "Leaving on a Jet Plane" and Joan Baez's "One Day at a Time."

A hymn had sustained me throughout the adoption process: "Be Not Afraid," by Father Bob Dufford of the St. Louis Jesuits. This wonderfully warm contemporary song of faith had given me hope and courage on the hardest days. Now on this Sunday, of all Sundays, the Cathedral guitar group sang it at Communion. I started to cry. I knew then that everything would work out.

Monday morning, the phone rang at the office.

"This is Kathy. When you come for dinner Wednesday, I'll have a child for you."

Kathy's beautiful home in northwest Washington was filled with Indian art. I met her adopted Indian daughter and son and her birth daughter. Kathy is an extraordinary person—warm, gracious, and caring. Her husband, a native of India, had died of cancer some years earlier. She had become involved in adoption work because she wanted a child and then wanted to help others adopt. Casually Kathy asked me what I would do if I found out I was pregnant.

"I'd probably say 'Hallelujah,' but I would still want this child," I replied.

She pulled out a packet of photos and sorted them into two piles.

"I haven't even looked at these yet," she said. "They just came."

These were the children she would be placing with families like us. I could have my pick of four children who had been baptized Catholic. Because Mother Teresa insisted that children who had been baptized be adopted by Catholics, Kathy reserved the others for non-Catholic families. My pile contained a three-year-old girl and three baby boys. All would find good homes.

I looked at the little girl. Even though we had thought "girl" all along, we wanted a baby. How do you pick your child from a photo the size of a man's thumb with no other information? All the babies were cute but the first picture touched something deep inside me. The boy had huge, sensitive, dark eyes. He looked scared but terribly alive. I kept peeking at him while we ate.

"This little guy speaks to me," I said, finally, handing the picture to Kathy. I had found our child.

I was thrilled and stunned. What would we do with a boy? What would we name him? Would Ron be pleased? I hoped I had picked the right child, then laughed. We would never know how the others turned out.

Ron was surprised but pleased with my news and immediately suggested a name: Rajeev. We would call him Raj. Of course! It fit the little guy in the photo and it had such a nice ring. Raj. Our Raj.

We were a long way from actually getting Raj, as I discovered when I read the instructions Kathy had given me. The Indian courts required a complicated dossier of notarized forms and certificates (birth, marriage, health, finances, employment) in triplicate with certificates authenticating the notaries. Air-mail postage alone cost more than sixty dollars.

The U.S. Immigration and Naturalization Service also required a complicated package of documents. When we finished the paperwork in late April, we settled down for more waiting. Summer recess delayed Indian court action for an extra month.

Finally in August 1981, the court gave us custody of Raj. I took the precious notification letter to INS so that final U.S. immigration processing could begin. We had made it!

In September, Kathy called with arrival information. In ten days the seemingly impossible would happen. We would have a *baby*.

Unlike some adoptive parents who decorate a child's room as soon as they finish the home study, we had done nothing to prepare for Raj's arrival. Looking at cute, empty furniture would only have made waiting more difficult. We spent a frantic weekend preparing the room, collecting and painting baby furniture, and buying supplies.

Even though Raj wasn't supposed to arrive until after 10:00 P.M., several close friends insisted on going to the airport with us. Loaded with cameras, they paced with us and shared our nervous anticipation.

When Raj's flight landed, we looked for a pretty young woman carrying a baby. Mother Teresa used off-duty Pan American and Eastern Airline hostesses to care for the children. It saved us airfare for an escort.

Then we saw them! Instants later, Raj was in my arms. I was beaming, but I didn't cry. Ron was hugging him, mugging outrageously. Raj was a little bewildered, but he didn't fuss or cry. He went to everyone and admired himself in the Polaroid pictures one of our friends took.

He was so beautiful! He had the incredible eyes of his picture and the most gorgeous thick black eyelashes I had ever seen. He was taller than we expected and barely fit the sleeper we had sent. He seemed extremely alert and healthy.

By 2:00 A.M., we had said farewell to the last of our friends and tried to put Raj to bed. He protested vigorously. Ron speculated that he had never slept in a bed. Of course it was also noon his time.

I tried to walk him to sleep. For four hours, we paced downstairs, but sleep would not come. No matter. As we clung to each other during that long, long night, something more important occurred. We bonded. By morning Raj had become *my* child. I had become his mother. The attachment was obvious to friends who visited later in the day.

The long road to adoption had ended. The longer road of child rearing had begun. We still had to finalize the adoption and have Raj made a citizen but who cared? Raj was ours at last, ours completely, ours forever.

From the first, Raj was an outgoing charmer with a smile that lights up his whole being. He changed our lives—but only for the better. The foreign students who thronged our home adored and spoiled him. He received so many stuffed animals that we speculated the toys were reproducing.

His grandparents on both sides were delighted. That first fall was a golden "high." How could we have lived without Raj? Today Raj is twelve and still a delight. He is a bright, sensitive, basically gentle boy whose life is full of friends, baseball, and basketball. He is slender and agile—a natural athlete who grows an inch and gains a pound while eating more than his father. He is crazy about his hamsters. He does well in school.

Occasionally we talk about his adoption. He has some curiosity about his birth mother and speculates about relatives he might have in India. We know as much as we ever will—I wish we knew more. He will just have to accept this gap. We have tried to make Raj proud of his Indian heritage without forcing it on him. He is an American and he wants to be like his buddies.

Still, the Indian art, music, food, and photos are around the house. It will be easy for him to learn more about his birth heritage whenever he wants to. We have numerous friends from India and Nepal and are seldom without a foreign student boarder. As for us, we are happy and grateful. I could not imagine a child I would rather parent.

## Shanti

From the moment Raj arrived, I was pretty sure I wanted a second child but I was in no hurry. As much as I adored Raj, I was continually exhausted for the first two years as I combined full-time work with motherhood. However, when he turned four and became easier to care for, the sense that it was time to adopt our second child became more insistent. On Mother's Day 1984, I decided that the time had come. Ron agreed. In Bangkok, our beautiful daughter-to-be was already a year old.

Preliminary checking showed that a new law had virtually closed India to foreign adoption. Our only option would have been a child with a handicapping condition who had been rejected by two Indian families. That wasn't for us. (The law has since been eased.)

The logical starting place should have been Holt International Children's Services' Omaha office, but I didn't think they would accept us because I needed to continue working.

Knowing that we needed to have our home study updated, we contacted another local agency, but were appalled when we were told to fill out a six-page form and submit to eighteen hours of interviews apiece. Eighteen hours? For an update?

I called the agency and told them to forget it. The social worker urged me to call Joan Worden at Holt. I had met Joan casually a couple of times. She had seemed like a good person. We were at a dead end. There was nothing to lose. Joan was warm and encouraging.

She bustled into our living room smiling and exclaimed over the beautiful Indian artworks. In her presence, it was impossible to remain pleasantly guarded as I had during the previous home study. She drew us out about our relationship with Raj and our hopes for a daughter. We showed her pictures of Raj with our relatives and with friends from around the world. I wondered when the update would start.

Joan pulled out our existing home study, glanced over it and announced that it hadn't done us justice. She could hardly wait to tell Holt's national office in Oregon about her "special family."

It was so wonderful to be treated with appreciation, dignity, and respect instead of feeling vaguely like someone on trial or a child playing power games with the teacher. I became a "Joan fan" on the spot—an admiration that has grown over the years.

We talked briefly about what countries to consider. If we couldn't adopt from India because of the new law, our next choice was Thailand. Ron has a sister-in-law from Thailand and we have several close Thai friends. Ron had been there several times and loved the country. Holt had a program in Bangkok, but it was small and adoption from Thailand is difficult.

Prospective parents had to be over thirty, never divorced, upper middle-class income, willing to travel to Bangkok, and have no more than one child of the opposite sex.

"By the time I read these rules, most people just say I'll take a Korean child," Joan said.

We said the rules didn't bother us. Besides, we'd love to go to Bangkok. We preferred to adopt from a country where we had ties, since our affinity for India had proved so helpful in raising Raj.

Joan suggested that we also apply for Brazil where Holt had just opened a new program. That was fine too. Several of our former Peace Corps friends had married delightful Brazilian women.

Periodically Joan called to update us on her search for our child. We filled out the Brazilian application forms complete with police check and fingerprints. In September, Joan told us we might hear something in November but that came and went due to summer court recess. We would have to wait until January.

In December, Joan called again.

"Are you still interested in Thailand?" she asked.

"Of course," I replied.

"I think I've found a little girl for you," she said. "I've put a hold on her. She wasn't even on our lists. I asked what was wrong with her, but they said everything is fine. She's just the age you want. Can you come out and look at her pictures?"

"I'll be there at four," I said in a daze.

I called Ron to tell him the startling good news. I tried unsuccessfully to contain my excitement. THIS WAS WONDERFUL!

Five hours later, I sat in Joan's office trembling as she handed me three pictures of a baby girl with enormous eyes and no hair. I knew we would say yes no matter what the pictures looked like but this child had a special presence.

Joan insisted that I take the photos home to Ron before officially accepting, but there was no doubt. We had found our daughter!

At home, Ron teased Raj about getting a bald sister, saying he didn't think we should take her unless we could be sure she would get hair. Raj immediately proposed naming her "Cyndall" after the girl in the film, *The Ewok Adventure*, which he had just seen. We gently told him that his sister's name would be Shanti (Peace), the name we had always said we would give a daughter. It seemed to fit her pictures. Were we in for a surprise!

Joan had given me the instructions for the voluminous paperwork that Thailand required and warned me to expect a long wait, maybe a year or even more. Despite my eagerness to get our daughter, that didn't bother me too much. The worst was over. We had another child. In time she would be ours.

I astonished Joan by completing the dossier in a day or so. The requirements were similar to India's, so I knew where to get everything. We sent the dossier to the Thai Consulate in Chicago and the U.S. State Department for approval before mailing the documents to Bangkok.

A slight hitch developed in Washington. The State Department would not approve our dossier because a form from the Nebraska Secretary of State's office carried an out-of-sequence date. The courier we had hired to expedite the process called to say he was returning the documents.

"What's the problem?" I asked, unable to believe that anything was seriously amiss. When he explained the difficulty, I relaxed.

"Could you just hold onto the stuff for a day or so? I'll call the Secretary of State's office and get a new form sent off right away," I said. I knew that my friend, Nebraska Secretary of State Allen Beermann, would expedite matters.

"Yeah, I'll hold 'em if you think this will work," the courier said dubiously.

I made a hasty call to Allen, who promised to send a new form by air express that afternoon. Half an hour later, the courier called back, sounding stunned.

"Boy, lady, you sure must be important," he said. "Your Secretary of State called me himself to make sure we got what we needed."

I didn't tell him that Allen had married one of my closest friends. Let the courier think I was important!

In a few days, our documents were returned with official seals. We sent them to Bangkok and settled in for what we had been warned might be a long wait.

We were pleased that our daughter was being cared for in a foster home instead of an orphanage. We felt the individual attention and love she was getting would be important to her development. Periodically we received photos (yes, she had grown hair!) and glowing reports on Shanti. A Holt worker from Iowa visited her for us and took more pictures. We could see she was being well cared for and living in a nice place.

In June 1985, Holt told us Shanti's name was not even on the list of children the Thai Welfare Department was processing. In July, a startled Holt worker in Oregon called. We had been approved before everyone else on the waiting list. We could go to Bangkok in October to get our daughter. We still don't know why our adoption was expedited.

By now Joan had left Omaha to join Holt's national staff. I

missed her warm guidance. The hardest struggle of this adoption was just ahead.

We had confirmed our travel plans with Holt in Oregon before purchasing our airline tickets. Ron planned to leave a week early to travel through Indonesia. We would meet in Bangkok. Raj would stay with my parents in California.

A week before Ron's departure, a Holt worker called and casually mentioned a hearing date—apparently unaware that it was two weeks after the date we had been given. I was thunderstruck. This couldn't be. The worker was sympathetic but said we couldn't get the schedule changed. Two departments of the Thai government were feuding over adoption procedures and we were caught in the middle.

I refused to believe nothing could be done. We had made our plans carefully and played by the rules. We had complex arrangements and a large sum of money at stake. I wasn't giving up without calling my congressman to see if he could get the appointment changed.

The worker wasn't pleased but finally admitted that the situation was causing problems for everyone. He warned me of the risks but said if I could get the thing straightened out, I would be doing everyone a favor.

A congressional staff member made two calls to Bangkok after eleven that night and got nowhere. She advised us that further pushing could endanger the adoption. We decided to make the best of a bad situation. Ron kept his tickets as they were and I exchanged mine for one with an open return. I would come home when I could.

Finally the big day arrived. Raj and I flew to California. Late on a Sunday night in early October, my dad drove me to the San Francisco Airport. The departure for Bangkok was a flight into the unknown—a trip halfway around the world with no definite date of return, to pick up a child who was a mystery to us.

During the long flight across the Pacific, I thought about what a magnificent success our gamble with Raj had been. I had a hunch this risk would pay off, too.

Ron met me at the Bangkok airport. Then we headed for the YWCA where Holt had placed us. Minutes after we arrived there, the phone rang. A Holt worker wondered if we would like to meet our daughter that afternoon. After an hour-long cab ride through Bangkok's picturesque, incredibly crowded streets, we arrived at Holt's simple but pleasant offices. Then we saw her.

A stunningly beautiful two-year-old girl with short, straight hair sat on the floor pounding blocks with a hammer. She was exquisitely dressed in a white dress, which accentuated her hair and enormous dark eyes. She looked like her pictures but much prettier. No camera could capture the elusive quality of her smile or her remarkable eyes.

I approached her gently and knelt beside her. She immediately began screaming. This one would take winning over. A social worker fussed with her and talked soothingly in Thai. Shanti continued to protest vigorously. Finally I held her for just a few minutes as we sat making awkward small talk with the social workers. Ron noticed how intently she watched us and sneaked glances at the pictures of Raj even as she pretended to be completely hostile.

We were in for five rough days with this bright, strong-willed child who knew what was happening and wanted no part of it. She was deeply attached to her foster mother, the only mother she had ever known. The woman obviously loved her deeply. We understood their agony and felt slightly guilty about it. However, we reminded ourselves that it was in Shanti's best interest to be adopted—and the foster mother had known from the beginning that this day would come.

We could see we had a spectacular daughter. She wouldn't reject us for long. Two-year-olds have very short memories. Her fight to stay with her foster mother was the healthy reaction of a child who had been greatly loved. She would soon transfer those feelings to us, especially when we left Bangkok.

Holt kept us busy getting to know Shanti, keeping appointments with government officials, and touring. We visited Shanti's home, an attractive middle-class townhouse with a television set and other electrical appliances. Her neighbors came out to inspect us. We could see that they all loved Shanti.

We also got the dates of required activities straightened out with no difficulty. I could have kept my original travel plans after all. However, reinstating the stops in Hong Kong and Hawaii would have cost too much so I booked a direct flight to San Francisco. This was probably a blessing. Touring with Shanti would have been an ordeal. We would be better off spending a quiet week with Raj and my parents.

At the required hearing with the Thai Welfare Board, Shanti sat on my lap screaming. Other foreign adoptive parents looked at us with pity. Their children from orphanages were silent, seemingly without reaction. I was thankful that our daughter showed such spirit. Her grief and anger were normal and understandable. When she got over them, we would have a magnificent addition to the family.

After several days, Pat, the social worker, let Shanti stay with us. As she explained to Shanti what had happened, Shanti raged. I had never seen such a tantrum. Then suddenly the worker started laughing. What was so funny?

"This one is so bright," Pat said. "She just asked me where your cars are. I told her in America. Then she asked me, 'What? Not even an auto ricksha?'"

Sustained close contact made Shanti, if anything, more resistant. In the hotel, she stood for hours in a corner facing the wall until she literally dropped.

She disliked Ron more than she disliked me, so he would chase her out of the corner when bedtime came, knowing she would seek protection with me. On street corners, she would wait until a crowd gathered, begin to weep and say loudly in Thai, "I want my mommy. I want to go home." In our room, she stared out the window gesturing in the direction she thought home was. We felt like child thieves.

The experience was bearable only because we understood how she felt and believed our adoption was in her best interest. Later we would regale her with tales of that week—of how she hated Daddy, of how she clung to the leg of a Marine from Cherokee, Iowa (about fifty miles from Omaha) at the U.S. Embassy, of how she refused to give money to an elephant at a cultural center we visited.

One week after my arrival, Shanti and I began our journey home. Ron would leave the next day for Hong Kong. As we kissed good-bye in the airport, Shanti seemed quiet, as if she realized she would never reclaim her home. I had dreaded the long flight without Ron, but it was surprisingly easy. Shanti was exhausted from the long week of battling us and slept almost the entire trip. Her resistance had collapsed. She seemed sad rather than defiant.

We arrived in San Francisco and stood in line with all the other immigrants to officially admit Shanti to the United States. My parents waited behind the barrier, impatient to meet their new granddaughter. Shanti took an instant liking to her grandmother—and vice versa. My mother's soft, gentle manner works wonders with most children.

Raj could hardly wait to meet his new sister. Early the next morning, he came in to greet both of us with kisses. Shanti socked him. It was an omen.

Shanti was tough. She had a steel will. She wouldn't sleep nights and screamed for hours at attempts to change her timetable. She wanted to sleep all afternoon and resisted efforts to keep her awake. This was expected but difficult.

She refused to smile or make friends with Raj or my brother's children. She watched everything intently. She missed nothing. On her first day in California, she uttered her first words in English, a complete sentence. Pointing to some peanuts, she echoed what she'd heard the other kids saying: "I want dat."

Mother and I exchanged glances. "Did you hear what I think I just heard?" I asked. Mother nodded. Within a month, Shanti was almost fluent in English.

It was enormously helpful to be with my parents during this stressful time. They could sometimes get Shanti to do things she wouldn't do for me. After a week in California, we picked up Ron in San Francisco and headed for home—despite Shanti's protests over saying good-bye to Grandma. We tried to tell her she would see her grandparents again, but we weren't sure she understood. On the plane from San Francisco to Salt Lake City, she stood in a corner in the rear facing the wall. It was Bangkok all over again.

Finally we arrived in Omaha where we were greeted by our dear friends Don and Gert Brodkey. They had brought treats and a balloon. Don's pictures show a bewildered little girl surrounded by beaming adults. At least we could now begin building our life together!

Raj personally gave Shanti a tour of our house. He showed her how to turn on the television. She began to seem less hostile. We thought she sensed that this was home. We noticed how intently she watched Raj and took cues from him.

She was still so sad-eyed that she could have posed for a CARE poster, but at least she was easier to handle. We took her everywhere—to our offices, to our congressman's office to thank them for the help, to Raj's school, to meet her new babysitter, and on errands.

Every day the gloom lightened a bit. She still wanted nothing to do with Ron, but it seemed to be getting harder and harder *not* to smile. I wondered how long she would ignore Daddy.

Ron played hard to get. He ignored Shanti and devoted himself to Raj. Finally one night, jealousy overcame resentment. Shanti shoved Raj off one of Ron's knees and claimed her place on his lap. We had won. Our beautiful daughter had joined our family.

From then on, progress was rapid. The sad-eyed waif was replaced by a beaming little girl with her very own "giggle" button. We soon got used to complete strangers stopping us to admire her beauty. Shanti remained cautious with strangers but became warm and uninhibited with relatives and friends.

She took my return to work in stride. She had seen me take Raj to school and pick him up. She realized that this was how we did things.

She quickly abandoned her Thai ways. She refused to do the ritual Thai greeting with bowed head and folded hands which had charmed everyone. She noticed that no one else was doing it and refused to perform. We had hoped she might retain a bit of her Thai language, but she soon forgot that too. When her Thai aunt spoke to her in Thai that Christmas, she showed no signs of comprehension.

She became very American. For her birthday, she wanted a Cabbage Patch Doll. When she saw Golden Arches, she would yell, "Yea McDonald's." She became a "Sesame Street" fan.

Today, Shanti is nine. She remains extremely bright, beautiful, and strong-willed. She's a top student and an avid reader. She has gained notoriety for her mastery of about one hundred world capitals her dad has taught her. She can beat almost any adult at computer Concentration.

Best of all, Shanti has developed into an affectionate child with a wonderful sense of humor. She's full of kisses and hugs for those she loves. She loves to hear the stories of our trip to Thailand. She giggles whenever she hears for the umpteenth time how she hated Daddy and how she hit Raj.

As I look at her growing and maturing, I see both the tiny, desperately unhappy child we brought home and the happy, confident, gifted girl of today.

Some days those memories are especially vivid. In 1991, Shanti made her First Communion, wearing a lovely white dress and veil, which her beloved godmother had worn. Proudly and confidently, she led the procession of families into the cathedral. Others saw a petite, extremely pretty girl who knew exactly what to do. I remembered a two-year-old in another white dress pounding blocks on a floor in Bangkok. Although I seldom cry, I fought back tears throughout the ceremony. How lucky we were and are!

Life with Shanti will always be a challenge. She'll usually have the answer while I'm trying to grasp the question. She will never bend easily to anyone else's will. But she will be a magnificent woman—a woman I will be incredibly proud to call my daughter.

CHAPTER 18

# Summary

Sometimes people ask us why it is necessary for Americans to adopt from overseas. Aren't there plenty of American children who need adoptive homes? Are Americans who adopt from other countries exploiting poor people?

We take such questions seriously because we know that they come from good people with a sincere concern for children. We suspect that these questions may occur to many adoptive parents.

We obviously believe there is a strong case for foreign adoption, or we wouldn't be devoting our lives to it or writing this book. A child who needs a loving home is a child who needs a loving home, whether she was born in Indianapolis or India. As foreign adoptive parents, we have learned that there are no national borders in affairs of the heart.

We cannot solve the economic and social problems of the Third World or the emerging nations of Eastern Europe. We are *absolutely opposed* to any adoption tainted by the slightest suspicion of baby selling. We advocate only the adoption of children whose futures were in the orphanages, foster homes, or streets of their native lands.

If our children had stayed where they were born, they would have faced bleak lives, deprived of not only the material goods we can provide, but also the greatest essential of all, a loving family of their own. Many of our children could not have received the health care they needed to overcome handicapping conditions. Others would never have had the opportunity to develop their gifts and talents. Who knows what these children will contribute because they have gained such opportunity? No one need ever apologize for reaching out to nurture and love a child, no matter where that child was born.

As to the question of why not adopt American children first, the answer is more complicated than the question. A great many people who adopt foreign children first explore domestic adoption and find out that it is extremely difficult unless they are willing and able to adopt a child with special needs. Domestic adoption is difficult because of:

- The shortage of healthy white infants available for adoption due to a combination of abortion and birth mothers keeping their children.
- The opposition of some minorities to the adoption of their children by white families.
- The fact that many children remain in foster care because of legal entanglements, not the unwillingness of foster parents or others to adopt. Until courts become more willing to sever parental rights, many children will continue to spend many years in the limbo of foster care.
- The desire of many families to adopt a healthy child rather than one who has physical, emotional, or mental problems. Many American children who are available for adoption have special needs. Parents who are not equipped to meet these needs should not attempt such adoptions.

It would be wonderful if more people were willing and able to adopt babies born with AIDS or crack addiction, but most adoptive parents are fairly ordinary people. They have neither the skills nor the resources to give such babies the special care they need.

Parenthood lasts a lifetime. It is not a project that merely requires people to be noble for a couple of weeks or months. No one should ever go into it with anything but the utmost realism about their own strengths and weaknesses. Most parents discover that even children without special needs or problems challenge them more than they ever thought possible.

A parent who would do very well with a child with no special needs might be unable to meet the needs of a child with certain handicapping conditions. The parent might even end up resenting the continuous demands, pressures, and expense—and thus the child who caused it all. This is *not* what adoption (foreign or domestic) is all about.

We see many benefits to the United States and other nations from encouraging foreign adoption. Foreign adopted children make the world even smaller. They enhance the concern of their adoptive parents about the developing world. This is especially true if the parents have traveled overseas to get their child. The parents' experience of working with people in another country will change them forever.

Foreign adopted children remain children of two cultures. They provide a bridge for greater understanding between their countries of origin and adoption. Eventually many of them will visit their countries of origin. Some, like Jodi, will even be reunited with their birth families. Others will see where they were born and find partial answers to their identity questions. With few exceptions, however, they will discover that they have become Americans. They may cherish their birth cultures (as they should), but they will remain Americans. They will enrich America with their special sense of mixed heritage. Their gifts, including their children, will make this nation a greater land for all Americans.

In closing, we would like to return to the road we invited you to walk with us at the start of this book. When we adopted our children, neither of us could have imagined how our lives would change. We are both infinitely richer in everything (but money) because we took the risks, fought the battles, and became parents to our children.

If you adopt, you will begin a wonderful lifetime adventure. You will meet treasured friends to share your journey. Your heart will expand in ways you never dreamed possible. You will know great joy and possibly great pain but, in most cases, the joy will outweigh the pain.

We began this book offering you a road of hope. Now you must walk this road if you think it is for you. Remember, there is only one child—and that child is all children. We pray that you find yours.

# CHAPTER 19

# Countries from Which Children Come

Americans considering adopting foreign-born children are naturally curious about the nations from which the children come. Once they select a country, they will want to begin studying that nation—learning more about its history, culture, and current conditions.

In this chapter, we present brief profiles of some of the nations from which most foreign adopted children come to the United States. For further information, contact your public library.

## COLOMBIA

**Capital:** Bogotá
**Population:** 33,600,000
**Location:** South America

Colombia is the fourth largest country in South America and the only nation bordered by both the Caribbean Sea and the Pacific Ocean. The western third of the country, where most of the people live, is mountainous. The country lies near the equator and the climate is mainly tropical.

Like most of South America, Colombia was colonized by the Spanish and that heritage is much in evidence today in the architecture of its cities, and in its language and culture. Nearly 60 percent of the people are of mixed Spanish and Indian descent. Some 20 percent are white, 14 percent mixed white and African descent, and 4 percent African descent. About 95 percent are Roman Catholics.

Colombia is a democracy that has good relations with the United States. The two nations have worked together to combat drug problems.

**Adoption Policies:** Adoptive parents must be at least twenty-five years old, married two years and have a gross family income of $20,000. They can have no more than one divorce per spouse. Single parents are not allowed. You are required to travel to Colombia for a minimum of two weeks.

## GUATEMALA

**Capital:** Guatemala City
**Population:** 9,500,000
**Location:** Central America

Guatemala is the most heavily populated and culturally distinctive country in Central America. Although it is small (42,042 square miles—about the size of Tennessee) it has several regions: southern highlands, tropical lowlands, and a coastal plain and piedmont zone. There are two mountain ranges. The climate is tropical, cooler in the highlands than in the hot, humid lowlands.

About 56 percent of the people are of mixed Indian and European ancestry while the remainder are Indians. Children range in color from white to light brown to darker shades of brown. They usually have dark brown or black hair and large dark eyes. The nation is predominantly Roman Catholic with some Protestants and some who practice the traditional Mayan religion. Guatemalans of Spanish heritage generally speak Spanish, but many Indians speak one of the Maya-Quiche languages. English is the second language of those who deal with foreigners in larger cities.

Guatemala is a democracy and enjoys good relations with the United States.

**Adoption Policies:** Adoptive parents must be at least twenty-five, married a minimum of two years and have no more than one divorce per spouse. They must have a gross family income of at least $20,000. Parents must travel to Guatemala for five to ten days. Children, who range in age from babies to older youngsters, normally come from government licensed orphanages. Adoptions can be done by proxy by a facilitator. Guatemala prefers couples, but some single parent adoptions are allowed.

## HONDURAS

**Capital:** Tegucigalpa
**Population:** 5,300,000
**Location:** Central America

Honduras, which is located in the center of Central America, is slightly larger than Tennessee. Most of the country is mountainous. The climate is subtropical in the lowlands and temperate in the mountains.

About 90 percent of the people are of mixed Indian and European descent. The remainder are Indian, white, and African descent. Most speak Spanish or Indian dialects. The people are overwhelmingly (97 percent) Roman Catholic. There is a small Protestant minority. Spanish and some Indian dialects are spoken. English is a second language of those who deal with foreigners in larger cities. Children range from white to light brown to some darker shades of brown. They have dark brown or black hair and large dark eyes.

Honduras, which has been troubled by border disputes with El Salvador and the generally unstable conditions of Central America, has been closely connected with the United States.

**Adoption Policies:** Adoptive parents must be at least twenty-five, married at least two years and have a gross family income of $20,000. They can have no more than one divorce per spouse. Honduras requires adoptive parents to make either one stay of several months or two shorter trips to appear before social workers. In some cases, parents might meet with government workers and social welfare officials. Adoption hostels (private homes) are available to accommodate adoptive parents. Since you will have your baby with you during much of your stay, pack as if you were taking a baby along. Bring plenty of diapers, bleach, and other supplies. These are difficult to obtain in Honduras. Single parents are allowed.

# INDIA

**Capital:** New Delhi
**Population:** 859,200,000
**Location:** Asia

India is one of the world's most heavily populated and fascinating countries. It is about one-third the size of the United States with three times its population. It is a complex and varied nation in every possible way. The climate varies from tropical monsoon in the south to temperate in the north.

India's people are as diverse as their land. There are fourteen official languages, including Hindi and English. Because of the linguistic diversity, English is an extremely common second language spoken by nearly all well-educated Indians. More than 80 percent of India's people are Hindus, 11 percent are Muslims, and the remainder are a mixture of Christians (both Protestant and Roman Catholic), Sikhs, Buddhists, and Jains. Children adopted from India range from very light brown to quite dark, depending on the region of their birth or ancestry. In general, north Indians tend to be lighter skinned than south Indians and Bengalis. Most have black hair and dark eyes.

India is the world's largest democracy and has been nonaligned since gaining its independence from Great Britain in 1947. It has a rich cultural history in music, art, and literature. It is home to some of the world's finest architecture, including the Taj Mahal.

**Adoption Policies:** India has complicated foreign adoption paperwork but does not require parents to go to the country. Parents must be twenty-five to forty years old, married at least two years with a gross family income of $20,000. Only couples may adopt. The paperwork includes numerous notarized forms to be approved by the Indian courts. Documents, however, do not need to be translated, as the language of the courts is English.

# SOUTH KOREA

**Capital:** Seoul
**Population:** 43,347,231
**Location:** Asia

177

This mountainous country, which is slightly larger than Indiana, is one of the most rapidly developing nations in Asia. Although most of the country consists of hills and mountains, there are wide coastal plains in the west and south. The climate is temperate with rainfall heavier in summer than winter.

Korea gained independence from Japan after World War II and was divided into two nations as part of the peace settlement. There has been a heavy American presence in Korea since the days of the Korean War. This accounts for part of Korea's rank as the largest source of foreign adopted children in the United States.

Korea's people are strongly homogeneous although there is a small Chinese minority. They have light brown skins, black hair, and dark, almond-shaped eyes. There is a strong Confucian tradition. Christians (both Protestant and Roman Catholic) comprise about 28 percent of the population. Buddhism and several folk religions are also found. The official language is Korean. English is widely taught in high schools.

**Adoption Policies:** Adoptive parents must be twenty-five to forty-five years old, married a minimum of three years, have a gross family income of $25,000 and no more than one divorce per spouse. Children are escorted to the United States. Parents are not required to travel there. If they go as escorts, there are many hotels. Only couples may adopt. Both infants and older children have been available, but the number of Korean children placed for adoption overseas is shrinking.

## NICARAGUA

**Capital:** Managua
**Population:** 3,900,000
**Location:** Central America

Nicaragua is one of the largest and poorest countries in Central America. For most of its history, it has experienced internal strife and wars with its neighbors. Most of its people are peasants who are concentrated along the Pacific side of the country. The terrain ranges from grasslands to the rugged Central Highlands formed by volcanic activity. The climate is tropical.

During most of the 1980s, Nicaragua was controlled by the Sandinista Party, which the United States strongly opposed. The U.S. economic boycott of the nation resulted in shortages of many commodities. With the defeat of the Sandinistas, normal relations with the United States have been restored but the country remains extremely poor.

About 70 percent of the people are of mixed white and Indian descent. Another 17 percent are white, 9 percent are of African descent, and 5 percent are Indian. Children range from white to various shades of brown and have dark brown or black hair and dark eyes. About 95 percent of the people are Roman Catholic. The rest are Protestant. The people are warm and caring. Spanish is the official language, but there are English and Indian-speaking minorities on the Atlantic coast.

**Adoption Policies:** Parents must be at least twenty-five years old with a gross family income of $20,000 and no more than one divorce per spouse. An Adoption Committee votes on all applications to adopt. Adoptable children are nearly always older or have special needs. Prospective parents must show how they are prepared to meet the special needs of the children. Adoption arrangements can be facilitated ahead of time. Parents must go to Nicaragua for seven to ten days. Single parents are accepted, but couples are preferred.

## PERU

**Capital:** Lima
**Population:** 22,000,000
**Location:** South America

Peru is a beautiful and varied land in northern South America. It is slightly smaller than Alaska. It includes a western coastal plain, rugged Andes Mountains, and an eastern lowland jungle of the Amazon Basin. The climate varies from tropical in the east to dry desert in the west.

Before its conquest by Spain, it was home of the famous Inca Indian civilization. Today the Inca ruins are international tourist attractions. Peru shares Lake Titicaca, the world's highest navigable lake, with Bolivia.

Nearly half of Peru's people are Indian. Some 37 percent are mixed white and Indian, 15 percent are white, 3 percent are African, Japanese, Chinese, or other heritages. The nation is predominantly Roman Catholic. Children range in appearance from light skinned to various shades of brown. They have dark brown or black hair and dark eyes.

The official languages are Spanish and Quéchua. Aymara, another Indian language, also is spoken.

**Adoption Policies:** Adoptive parents must be at least thirty years old, married two years, have a gross family income of $20,000 and no more than one divorce per spouse. They must either make one trip that lasts six to eight weeks or two shorter trips. Adoptions are facilitated by Peruvian lawyers. Parents must appear before government officials. Many children are relinquished by their mothers at birth, so infants are available. Either couples or single parents may adopt.

## PHILIPPINES

**Capital:** Manila
**Population:** 64,906,990
**Location:** Off coast of Southeast Asia

The Philippines is a chain of more than seven thousand islands and islets lying about five hundred miles off the southeast coast of Asia. The total land mass is slightly larger than Arizona. The nation is mountainous and subject to damaging volcanic activity. The climate is tropical. There is abundant rainfall in most of the nation.

The Philippines was a U.S. colony prior to World War II. The islands have a democratic government.

The people of the Philippines are mostly Malay, although there is a Chinese minority. They have brown skin, black hair, and dark almond-shaped eyes.

More than 80 percent are Roman Catholics. There are Protestant, Muslim, and Buddhist minorities. The official languages of the country are Filipino (based on Tagalog) and English.

**Adoption Policies:** Adoptive parents must be twenty-five to forty years old, married three years, have a gross family income of $20,000 and no more than one divorce per spouse. Babies and older children are available for adoption. Most are in orphanages run by the Department of Social Services. Children are escorted to the United States. There is no need for parents to travel to the islands. Single parents are only permitted to adopt children over five years of age with special needs.

## THAILAND

**Capital:** Bangkok
**Population:** 58,800,000
**Location:** Southeast Asia

Thailand is one of Asia's most rapidly developing nations and a longtime ally of the United States. This kingdom is one of the few nations in Asia that was never colonized. Thais are intensely proud of their country and this heritage. This is extremely important for adoptive parents to remember in all their dealings with Thailand.

This is a beautiful, fertile land with a rich culture. The climate is tropical. More than 95 percent of Thailand's people are Buddhist. Most of the rest are Muslim. Christians and others are less than 1 percent of the population. There are numerous beautiful Buddhist pagodas, temples, and shrines throughout the country. About 80 percent of the Thai people are literate. English is the second language of the elite. It is commonly spoken, also, by taxi drivers, hotel personnel, and merchants in Bangkok. The people range in color from very light brown to darker browns. They tend to have large, dark eyes that are just slightly slanted. Thai women are often considered to be among the most beautiful in the world.

Thailand has a per capita income of $1,160. Health and nutrition conditions are better than in most of the region. However, the influx of refugees from war-torn neighboring countries has strained resources.

Bangkok is one of the world's most interesting and cosmopolitan cities. Visitors should take extra money to purchase souvenirs—especially silks, jewelry, and clothing. Thai food is delicious and distinctive. It resembles Chinese food, but tends to be spicier. American food is readily available in Bangkok.

**Adoption Policies:** Adoptive parents must be thirty years old, married five years unless there is infertility, have no divorces and a gross family income of $30,000. Children are not freed for adoption until they are at least a year old and processing normally takes at least a year after that. The youngest Thai children available for adoption are toddlers. Only married couples may adopt. One trip of seven to ten days is required.

# CHAPTER 20

# International Adoption Agencies by State

The following list of adoption agencies was provided by The International Children's Concerns Committee. Check your telephone book for phone numbers and addresses. States are included only when an agency is based in a city outside the listed state.

**ALABAMA**
Villa Hope, *Birmingham*

**ALASKA**
Adoption Advocates International, *Port Angeles, WA*
Adoption Services of WACAP, *Seattle, WA*
Fairbanks Adoption and Counseling, *Fairbanks*

**ARIZONA**
Dillon Southwest, *Scottsdale*
Globe International Adoptions, Inc., *Glendale*
House of Samuel, *Tucson*
Jewish Family and Children's Home, *Phoenix*

**ARKANSAS**
None listed

**CALIFORNIA**
AASK America/Aid to Adoption of Special Kids, *San Francisco*
Adopt, Inc., *San Carlos*
Adopt International, *San Carlos*

Adoption Horizons, *Eureka*
Adoption Services International, *Ventura*
Adoptions Unlimited, *Chino*
Bal Jagat, *Chatsworth*
Bay Area Adoption Services, Inc., *Cupertino*
Catholic Charities, *San Francisco*
Catholic Social Services, *San Francisco*
Children's Home Society of California, *San Jose* (Main Office—
with 17 offices in north and north central California)
Chrysalis House, *Fresno*
Family Connections, *Modesto*
Family Network, Inc., *Marina*
Help the Children, Inc., *Stockton*
Holt International Children's Services, *Lakewood and San Leandro*
Life Adoption Services, *Tustin*
Partners for Adoption, *Santa Rosa*
Sierra Adoption Services, *Nevada City*
Vista del Mar, *Los Angeles*

## COLORADO
Adoption Alliance, *Aurora*
Bethany Christian Services, *Denver*
Colorado Adoption Center, *Fort Collins, Wheatridge*
Friends of Children of Various Nations (FCVN), *Denver*
Hand-In-Hand, *Colorado Springs*

## CONNECTICUT
The Brightside, *West Springfield, MA*
Family Service, Inc., *Bristol, New Britain*
International Alliance for Children, *New Milford*
Jewish Family Services of New Haven, *New Haven*
New Beginnings Family & Children's Services, Inc., *Mineola, NY*
Wide Horizons for Children, Inc., *New Britain*

## DELAWARE
The Adoption Agency, *Wilmington*

Child and Home-Study Associates, *Wilmington*
Welcome House, *Doylestown, PA*

## DISTRICT OF COLUMBIA
Adoption Service Information Agency (ASIA), *Washington*
American Adoption Agency, *Washington*
Barker Foundation, *Washington*
Children's Adoption Support Services, Inc., *Washington*
Datz Foundation, *Washington*
International Families, Inc., *Washington*
Lutheran Social Services (DC), *Washington*
Welcome House, *Doylestown, PA*
World Child, *Washington*

## FLORIDA
The Adoption Center, *Maitland*
Creative Adoptions, Inc., *Orlando*
Jewish Family and Community Services, *Jacksonville*
Lutheran Social Services of NE Florida, *Jacksonville*
Suncoast International Adoptions, Inc., *Indian Rocks Beach*
Universal Aid for Children, Inc., *Miami Shores*

## GEORGIA
Child Services and Family Counseling, *Atlanta*
Holston United Methodist Homes for Children,
 *Greeneville, TN*
Homes for Children, *Atlanta*
Illien Adoptions International Ltd., *Atlanta*
Lutheran Ministry of Georgia, *Atlanta*
My Turn Now, *Atlanta*

## HAWAII
Hawaii International Child Placement & Family Services, Inc.,
 *Honolulu*

## IDAHO
Adoption Services of WACAP, *Seattle, WA*
Idaho Youth Ranch Adoption Services, *Boise*

185

## ILLINOIS
Bensenville Home Society, *Bensenville*
Bethany Christian Services, *Evergreen Park*
Catholic Charities, *Chicago*
Children's Home and Aid Society of Illinois, *Rockford*
Family Network, Inc., *Edwardsville*
Family Service of Decatur, *Decatur*
Love Basket, *Hillsboro, MO*
Lutheran Social Services of Illinois, *Chicago*
Sunny Ridge Family Center, *Wheaton*
Travelers' and Immigrants' Aid, *Chicago*
Universal Adoption Services, *Jefferson City, MO*

## INDIANA
Americans for African Adoptions, Inc., *Indianapolis*
Bethany Christian Services, *Indianapolis*
Coleman Adoption Services, *Indianapolis*
Sunny Ridge Family Center, *Highland*

## IOWA
Hillcrest Family Services, *Cedar Rapids*
Holt International Children's Services, *Carter Lake*
Kids Each Served in Love (KESIL), *Omaha, NE*
Sunny Ridge Family Center, *Wheaton, IL (and eastern Iowa)*

## KANSAS
Children's Foundation—Adoption and Counseling, Inc.,
   *Louisburg*
Gentle Shepherd, *Olathe*
International Adoption & Counseling Service of Kansas,
   *Shawnee*
Universal Adoption Services, *Jefferson City, MO*

## KENTUCKY
Children's Home of Northern Kentucky, *Covington*

## LOUISIANA
Children's Bureau of New Orleans, *New Orleans*

# MAINE
Growing-Thru-Adoption, *Lewiston*

# MARYLAND
American Adoption Agency, *Washington, D.C.*
Associated Catholic Charities of Baltimore, *Baltimore*
Barker Foundation, *Washington, D.C.*
Children's Adoption Support Services, Inc., *Washington, D.C.*
Concern, *Fleetwood, PA*
Datz Foundation, *Washington, D.C.*
Family and Children's Society, *Baltimore*
Option of Adoption, *Philadelphia, PA*
Welcome House, *Doylestown, PA*

# MASSACHUSETTS
Alliance for Children, *Wellesley*
Beacon Adoption Center, *Great Barrington (area code 413 only)*
Cambridge Adoption and Counseling Associates, Inc.,
    *Cambridge, Watertown*
Florence Crittenton League, *Lowell*
Love the Children, *Quakertown, PA*
Lutheran Child and Family Services of Massachusetts,
    *Worcester*
Protestant Social Service Bureau, Inc., *Wollaston*
The Brightside, *West Springfield*
Wide Horizons for Children, Inc., *Waltham*

# MICHIGAN
Alternative Adoption Advisors, *Augusta*
Americans for International Aid and Adoption, *Birmingham*
Bethany Christian Services, *Grand Rapids, Madison Heights*
Children's Hope, *Shepherd*
Foreign Adoption Consultants, *Kalamazoo*
Morning Star Adoption Resource Services, Inc., *Royal Oak*

# MINNESOTA
Children's Home Society of Minnesota, *St. Paul* ·
Crossroads, *Minneapolis*
Forever Families International Adoption Agency, *Eveleth*

Hope International Family Services, Inc., *Stillwater*
Jewish Family Service of St. Paul, *St. Paul*
Lutheran Social Services, *Minneapolis*

## MISSISSIPPI
None listed

## MISSOURI
Adoption Associates, *St. Louis*
Adoption Resource Center/R&R Health Services, *St. Louis*
Catholic Charities, *Kansas City, KS*
Children's Foundation-Adoption and Counseling, Inc.,
  *Kansas City*
Family Network, Inc., *St. Louis*
International Adoption & Counseling Service of Kansas,
  *Shawnee, KS*
Love Basket, *Hillsboro*
Lutheran Family and Children's Services of Missouri, *St. Louis*
Universal Adoption Services, *Jefferson City*
Worldwide Love for Children, *Springfield*

## MONTANA
Montana Intercountry Adoption, *Bozeman*

## NEBRASKA
Child Savings Institute, *Omaha*
Holt International Children's Services, *Carter Lake, IA*
Kids Each Served in Love (KESIL), *Omaha*
Lutheran Family Services, *Omaha*

## NEVADA
Nevada State Welfare (check county name in phone book)

## NEW HAMPSHIRE
Wide Horizons for Children, Inc., *Concord*

## NEW JERSEY
A.M.O.R., *Matawan*
The Adoption Agency, *Haddonfield*

Adoptions International, Inc., *Philadelphia, PA*
Casa del Mundo, Inc., *Clark*
Child and Home-Study Associates, *Media, PA*
Children of the World, *Glen Ridge*
Family and Children's Counseling and Testing Center, *Elizabeth*
Growing Families, Inc., *Lincroft and Morristown*
Holt International Children's Services, *West Trenton*
Homestudies, Inc., *Teaneck*
Jewish Family and Children's Services, *Philadelphia, PA*
Love the Children, *Quakertown, PA*
Lutheran Social Services, *Trenton*
New Beginnings Family & Children's Services, Inc., *Mineola, NY*
Tabor Children's Services, *Doylestown, PA*
Welcome House, *Doylestown, PA*

## NEW MEXICO
Rainbow House/Friends of Children of Various Nations, *Belen*

## NEW YORK
Adoption Alliance, *Sayville*
Adoption and Counseling Service, Inc., *Syracuse*
Adoptions International, Inc., *Philadelphia, PA*
Community Maternity Services, *Albany*
Evangelical Adoption and Family Service, Inc., *Syracuse*
Family Focus Adoption Services, *Little Neck*
Family Service of Westchester, Inc., *White Plains*
International Alliance for Children, *New Milford, CT*
Roberta Kalmar, *Brooklyn*
Love the Children, *Quakertown, PA*
Lund Family Center, *Burlington, VT (for near the VT border)*
New Beginnings Family & Children's Services, Inc., *Mineola*
New York Home-Study Service, *Westbury*
Parsons Child and Family Center, *Albany*
Spence-Chapin, *New York*
Voice for International and Domestic Adoption (VIDA), *Hudson*
Wide Horizons for Children, Inc., *Ronkonkoma*

## NORTH CAROLINA
Bethany Christian Services, *Asheville*

189

Christian Adoption Services, *Matthews*
Lutheran Family Services, *Raleigh*

## NORTH DAKOTA
New Horizons, *Bismarck*

## OHIO
Family Counseling and Crittenton Services, *Columbia*
Foreign Adoption Consultants, *Macedonia*
Gentle Care, *Columbus*
Jewish Family Service, *Sylvania*
Lutheran Social Services of Central Ohio, *Columbus*
Lutheran Social Services of the Miami Valley,
    *Dayton and Cincinnati*

## OKLAHOMA
The Adoption Center, *Bartlesville*
Dillon International, Inc., *Tulsa*
Project Adopt, *Oklahoma City*
Small Miracles International, Inc., *Midwest City*
United Methodist Counseling Services, *Oklahoma City*

## OREGON
Holt International Children's Services, *Eugene*
Plan International Adoption Services, *McMinnville*

## PENNSYLVANIA
The Adoption Agency, *Ardmore and Lancaster*
Adoption Alliance, *Warrington*
Adoption Services, *Camp Hill*
Adoptions International, Inc., *Philadelphia*
Child and Home-Study Associates, *Media*
Concern, *Fleetwood*
Jewish Family and Children's Services, *Philadelphia*
Keystone Adoption Services, *Wilkes-Barre*
Love the Children, *Quakertown*
Lutheran Children and Family Service, *Philadelphia*
Lutheran Service Society of Western Pennsylvania,
    *Greensburg*

Option of Adoption, *Philadelphia*
Pearl S. Buck Foundation, *Perkasie*
Tabor Children's Services, *Doylestown and Philadelphia*
Today's Adoption Agency, *Hawley*
Welcome House, *Doylestown*

## RHODE ISLAND
Alliance for Children, *Pawtucket*
Wide Horizons for Children, Inc., *Waltham, MA*

## SOUTH CAROLINA
Bethany Christian Services, *Greenville*

## SOUTH DAKOTA
Holt International Children's Services, *Carter Lake, IA*
Kids Each Served in Love (KESIL), *Omaha, NE*

## TENNESSEE
Holston United Methodist Homes for Children, *Greeneville*

## TEXAS
Adoption Resource Consultants, *Richardson*
Adoption Services, Inc., *Ft. Worth*
Adoption Services Unlimited, *De Soto*
Child Placement Center, *Killeen*
Covenant Children, *Dallas*
Dillon International, Inc., *Tulsa, OK*
Los Niños International, *Dallas, San Antonio*
Quality of Life, *Dallas*

## UTAH
Adoption Services of WACAP, *Seattle, WA*
Children's House International, *Salt Lake City*

## VERMONT
AASK Northeast Rootwings, *Barre*
Lund Family Center, *Burlington*
Vermont Children's Aid Society, *Winooski*

86377

## VIRGINIA
American Adoption Agency, *Richmond*
Barker Foundation, *Washington, D.C.*
Catholic Charities of Richmond, *Richmond*
Catholic Charities of South-Western Virginia, *Roanoke*
Datz Foundation, *Vienna*
Family Services of Tidewater, Inc., *Norfolk (Main Office)*
Holston United Methodist Homes for Children, *Greeneville, TN*
Welcome House, *Doylestown, PA*

## WASHINGTON
Adoption Advocates International, *Port Angeles*
Adoption Services of WACAP, *Seattle*
Catholic Community Services, *Seattle*
Travelers Aid Adoption Service, *Seattle*

## WEST VIRGINIA
Burlington United Methodist Child Placement Services, *Scott Depot*
Catholic Charities of South-Western Virginia, *Roanoke, VA*
Children's Home Society of West Virginia, *Charleston, Princeton and Morgantown*
Comprehensive Studies, *Charleston*

## WISCONSIN
Adoption Services of Green Bay, *Green Bay*
Bethany Christian Services, *Waukesha*
Community Adoption Center, *Janesville, Madison, Manitowoc*
Division of Community Services, *Madison*
Hope International Family Services, Inc., *Stillwater, MN*
Lutheran Social Services of Wisconsin and Upper Michigan, *Madison, Milwaukee*
New Horizons, *Bismarck, ND*
Pauquette Children's Services, *Portage*
Sunny Ridge Family Center, *Green Bay*

## WYOMING
Holt International Children's Services, *Carter Lake, IA*